BETWEEN LIGHT AND SHADOW

BETWEEN LIGHT
AND SHADOW

A Guatemalan Girl's Journey through Adoption

JACOB WHEELER ⊁ Foreword by Kevin Kreutner

University of Nebraska Press ⊁ Lincoln and London

LIBRARY OF CONGRESS Cataloging-in-Publication Data
Wheeler, Jacob, 1978–
Between light and shadow: a Guatemalan girl's journey
through adoption / Jacob Wheeler; foreword by Kevin Kreutner.
p.   cm.   Includes bibliographical references.
ISBN 978-0-8032-3362-1 (cloth: alkaline paper)
   1. Intercountry adoption—Guatemala—Case studies.
   2. Intercountry adoption—United States—Case studies.
   3. Adopted children—Guatemala—Case studies.
   4. Adopted children—United States—Case studies. I. Title.
HV875.58.G9W44 2011   362.734092—dc22   2010029590

FRONTIS: Ellie Walters visited the Mayan ruins at Kabáh
in Mexico's Yucatán peninsula after she was adopted by Bob and
Judy Barrett-Walters and before her return to Guatemala. Photo
courtesy of the Barrett-Walters family.

SET IN ADOBE GARAMOND PRO BY BOB REITZ.
DESIGNED BY A. SHAHAN.

Este libro está dedicado a todas las madres de Guatemala.

Contents

Foreword

Back in my days as a radical college newspaper opinion columnist, a professor once pointed out to me that very few things in life are black-and-white. Although I have retained much of that radical fervor, I have learned that my professor was correct and nowhere more so than when it comes to all things related to adoptions from Guatemala.

During the peak periods of adoptions from Guatemala, I served as the chief writer for GuatAdopt.com. For a number of reasons—luck, integrity, and experience—GuatAdopt.com became the most popular and relied-upon source of news and information for those interested or involved in Guatemalan adoptions. Inasmuch as the site publicly served a vital role, behind the scenes I came to understand the extent to which everything in adoptions was a shade of gray.

An adoption professional once told me, "At its best, there is no adoption system as good as Guatemala's. At its worst, there is none worse." This statement most accurately describes what I have experienced after counseling hundreds if not thousands of families going through adoptions, both smooth sailing and challenged, from Guatemala.

With this story, Jacob Wheeler has documented just one of the myriad adoption stories that exist while also chronicling an amazing reunion. Although this one story can in no way be used to characterize or stereotype the tens of thousands of adoptions from Guatemala, it is a testament to many. What it does is examine the real complexities of the institution of intercountry adoption—where well-meaning and sometimes humanitarian first world wealth collides with the extreme poverty, despair, misogyny, racism, and violent history of Guatemala.

Many nongovernmental organizations (NGOS) and government institutions make the claim that poverty is not a valid reason for intercountry adoption. In a perfect world, this is a very true statement. But equally true is that no woman should ever find herself in the position of having to make the difficult decision to relinquish a child she loves because of poverty. Absent of social programs, civil liberties, welfare, education, and the like, this school of thought lacks merit beyond philosophical rhetoric. The truth is that thousands of woman have faced this decision, and if it were not for legal barriers around the globe that essentially ban the option, without providing an alternative, hundreds of thousands if not millions more could face this decision.

Although intercountry adoption is by no means a solution to the woes facing impoverished children and women globally, it does go to show just how badly solutions are needed. As one reads this story, it is crucial that they realize its characters are not unique and that the situations in which they find themselves are more the rule than the exception in many parts of the globe.

Adoptive parents come in all shapes, sizes, colors, religions, philosophies, and mind-sets. In honor of this, I urge some caution to resist the temptation to characterize us all by the limited sample of adoptive parents Jacob Wheeler has touched. Many adoptive parents go through great pains to learn their children's history, honor it, and do all that is possible to maintain their children's roots and sense of identity as *chapines* (Guatemalans). All around the country exist local support and social groups where adoptive families unite to celebrate their family roots. They also join together to support causes that focus on helping children and families in Guatemala.

Last, respect is essential in any examination of the dynamics of intercountry adoption. It is impossible for those of wealth, comfort, and education to comprehend all that permeates the socioeconomics and culture of a poor, struggling mother in Guatemala. Those who have never suffered through infertility cannot fathom the mind-set of the prospective or in-process adoptive parent. And most important, we must all have deep respect for the Guatemalan children who have joined families in the United States through adoption. They are not to blame or applaud for the legacy of the institution that brought so much change to their lives. They each have their own questions, feelings, perspectives, and privacy concerns that should be respected above all else.

Kevin Kreutner

?֍ Preface

This is a true story, to the best of my ability to tell it. The reader should be aware, however, that some dialogue and scenes in the first half of the book, before I entered the picture as a documentarian and translator, are re-created based on interviews with the primary characters. I handled it this way to make their story come alive on the page. Also, the names of certain characters have been changed to protect their identities or the safety of others in the story.

Readers will notice a different authorial voice used in the book's two parts, "The Journey" and "The Return," which I hope is not too jarring. I use a journalistic tone in the prologue to introduce the reader to the debate over Guatemalan adoption, its myriad sides, some of its key players, and the historical background that led to this unique debate. "The Journey" is written in the past tense and features narrative nonfiction and a touch of dramatic realism. Finally, "The Return" is written in the present tense, uses a first-person narrative, and appeals to the tools of a documentarian and ethnographer.

Although I struggled with the first-person voice, I thought it only fair to make myself a primary character once I began driving the action. But this is no memoir. I am not a social worker, nor have I adopted a child, nor do I call Guatemala my homeland, which is why I felt most comfortable when I could observe and report. This is not my story—it belongs to Ellie, Antonia, Judy, and, perhaps, all children adopted from Guatemala.

A book published by a university press in the United States is typically written for an academic audience, typically stands on the shoulders of primary sources and existing works written about the subject, and typically establishes the author as a qualified expert on that subject. This is not that kind of book. *Between Light and Shadow* is not academic because I seek to reach a much broader audience. The book does not scale a mountain of primary sources because, when it comes to the perspectives of Guatemalan women who have given up their children for international adoption, there are few. The resources to tell Ellie's story were found not in a library but in the remote town of Tiquisate. And I am no authority in this field. The experts—whether rich or poor, literate or illiterate—are those who have experienced Guatemalan adoption. As these adoptees come of age in the United States, I only hope that they will enjoy this book and that it will inspire them to explore their own journeys.

❦

It was in the fall of 2003 that I first set foot in Guatemala, and at the Proyecto Lingüístico Quezalteco (PLQ) in the highland city of Quetzaltenango (Xela), Guatemala's second-largest city, that I fell in love with this country, its people, their languages, culture, mountains, lakes, and tragic history. Nominally, PLQ is a language school—one of the best in Central America and one that offers a genuine cultural immersion (that is, it is better than studying in touristy Antigua)— but PLQ is also a study in past and present Guatemalan politics and history and, from a progressive angle, the perspective of those who for centuries have been denied a voice: *campesinos, indígenas, activistas, feministas, guerrilleros.* Photos of Che Guevara, Salvadoran archbishop Oscar Romero, and Guatemala's martyred priests, nuns, and *hermanos* line the walls here. Some of the teachers at PLQ were involved in the guerrilla fighting during Guatemala's civil war. Inspiring. As such, I am not the first PLQ alum to publish a book about Guatemala, and I won't be the last. The language skills, cultural knowledge, and political activism that PLQ gave me birthed this book. Special thanks goes to Carlos Sanchez, Eduardo Elias, Brenda Morales, Miriam at La Escuela de la Montaña, and others in Xela, especially Jessica Ohana Gonzalez, one of the strongest people I know.

An early version of this book became my graduate school thesis for a master's degree in creative nonfiction from Goucher College near Baltimore. For the inspiration to write, report, document, narrate, and edit, and for giving me those all-important deadlines, I thank Patsy Sims, Kevin Kerrane, Pete Earley, Philip Gerard, and, especially, Suzannah Lessard. Thanks to all who helped edit, market, critique, and put my Guatemalan experience in perspective: my agent for a time, Anna Stein; my parents, Norm and Mimi Wheeler, and my sister, Julia; Anne-Marie Oomen; Ruth Gilmer, David Hendricks, and the Sunday-night sauna crew; Doug Stanton; James Coleman; Cindy Garner; Joshua Lang; Waleed Al-Shamma; Leif Utne; Christian Avila; Peter Payette and Interlochen Public Radio; *In These Times* publisher Joel Bleifuss and my former colleagues Sanhita Sinha Roy and Brian Cook; Kevin Kreutner; countless others who offered suggestions and support via e-mail; folks at Curbstone Press and Penn State University Press who offered me helpful ghost edits even though they did not publish this book; and Matt Bokovoy, Sabrina Stellrecht, Annette Wenda, and the University of Nebraska Press for finally leading this project home. Above all, thanks to *mi querida* Sarah, for your patience during my years of gallivanting around Central America. Yes, above all, your patience.

Throughout 2005 I interviewed more than twenty American families who were in various stages of adopting, or had adopted, from Guatemala. Most hailed from Michigan, but also Ohio, Minnesota, Tennessee, and California. Though most are not mentioned in this story (and some wanted to remain anonymous), their perspectives, tears, and laughter greatly informed my studies of this journey: my time with them was essential. Thanks, in alphabetical order, to Judy, Bob, and Ellie (Beneríce) Barrett-Walters; Jill, Willis, Cony, and Sara Bentgen; Steve and Judy Burns; Nancy Bykerk; Don and Marilyn Floyd; Harry and Juliana Fried and Allison Stupka; Shelley Greene; April and Kenny Hayman; Steve and Lisa Hinz-Johnson; Terry and Kim Lamb; April Ogden; Kathy O'Neill; Tom and Ham Reynoso; Steve and Elizabeth Sorenson; Leif, Cilla, and Mateo Utne; and Karen and Bill Weis.

I also interviewed adoption social workers, advocates, attorneys, activists, journalists, owners of *hogares*, ministers and missionaries, heads of nonprofits, and one Guatemalan first lady. It is inevitable that some will object to the way I portray Guatemalan adoption or their role therein. Nevertheless, I am extremely grateful for the time they spent with me, the viewpoints they conveyed, and the doors they opened. I will name a few, again in alphabetical order: Sandy Al-Shamma, Patrick Atkinson from the God's Child Project, Nancy Bailey from Semillas de Amor, former first lady Wendy de Berger, Tracy Bonn, Hanley Denning and Safe Passage, Hector Dionisio and Casa Alianza, Blanca Estela and Guatemalan Roots, Nancy Fox, Dora Giusti and UNICEF, Hands Across the Water, Ellen Herman, Alan Keener, Kevin Kreutner who edits the wonderfully informative and balanced Web site GuatAdopt.com, Tim Nelson, Betsie and Brad Norris, Jaime Tecú, Enrique Toledo, Cher Cronican Walker, and Hannah Wallace. Once again, thank you.

BETWEEN LIGHT AND SHADOW

❧ Prologue

This is a story about the journey of a girl to the United States from the desperate, poor streets of her home village in Guatemala. It's about the birth mother who gave her up for adoption because she was pressured and promised money by the lawyers who make Guatemalan adoption so lucrative and so controversial. It is a story about one American family and its journey through international adoption: the guilt, the joy, the premonitions, and the conflicts that unfolded when the characters traveled to Central America and wealth met poverty head-on. It's also a story about a very poor nation divided by race and class and a bloody history that continues today—and how its people deal with the humiliating perception that the world wants Guatemala more for its children than anything else it has to offer.

Finally, this is a story about digging up one's past and returning to the place where the journey began. It's about a girl's reunion with her birth mother many years later: love and heartbreak, betrayal and redemption, murder and witchcraft, confronting abandonment, and what it means to be wealthy while surrounded by the poor.

This story examines the claim that Guatemalan adoption is a supply-and-demand industry where the arbiters are constantly profiting from the vulnerability of the country's downtrodden and hungry mothers. But it also casts Guatemalan adoption as the impetus for a wonderful journey from rags to riches that, until recently, gave thousands of children every year lives and opportunities they would never have had if they were not relinquished early in their lives. Although political battles play out in Washington DC and Guatemala City over whether to keep this particular international adoption window open, this story does not intend to take sides or tell the reader whether Guatemalan adoption is right or wrong, just or unjust, legal or illegal. This conversation is far too complicated to be judged in absolutes. And whether Guatemalan adoption reopens and returns to the peak level it reached in 2007 or not, abuses in foreign adoption are nowhere near resolute, giving this case study relevance for years to come.

Adoption from Haiti flooded the news after an Idaho church group unwisely and illegally attempted to smuggle Haitian children into the Dominican Republic following the disastrous earthquake in early 2010. And the U.S. media focused on adoption from Russia after an adoptive mother moronically sent her child on a one-way flight back to Moscow. Guatemalan adoption may someday return to the front page, too.

This story should not be interpreted as the typical journey through Guatemalan adoption. It is merely a glimpse into the life of one girl, Ellie Walters in Michigan, whose window between her Guatemalan past and her American present happens to be more open than most. Ellie is a bicultural kid, a minority because of her skin color, though she spent her formative years with a privileged white family. In the global age, she is a rare example of an intermediary between rich and poor, between present and past.

❧

Until recently, almost every flight leaving Guatemala City for the United States had one: a tiny brown baby held in the arms of her white parents, many of whom were not able to have their own biological children, and so, for them, these moments of pure joy were the culmination of years of anxious waiting. For these adoptive parents, the airplane ride, the visit to the American Embassy to acquire the child's visa, and the baby handoff in the busy lobby in one of the capital's Americanized hotels replaced a maternity ward or a private home as the point of initial contact with their son- or daughter-to-be.

This beautiful yet strange scene of the foster mother and the Guatemalan attorney passing a baby to its new adoptive parents in the sterile lobby of the Marriott or the Radisson or the Camino Real near the American Embassy became an everyday occurrence here. Until 2008 Guatemala held the distinction of being the only Latin American country that did not recognize the United Nations Hague Convention on Protection of Children and Cooperation in Respect of Intercountry Adoption of 1993 that pushes for stringent state control over international adoptions. The Guatemalan Constitution has traditionally prevented international treaties from superseding the country's domestic laws, and until 2008 adoptions in Guatemala fell under the notary system, which meant that they were essentially privatized and run by lawyers and judges who had plenty to choose from when it came to impoverished, malnourished, and sometimes abandoned or stolen babies.

But advocates argue that Guatemala's distinction also made it the point of departure for a wonderful journey that gave thousands of children every year lives and opportunities with loving families of financial means in the richest country in the world—whereas elsewhere in Latin America, countries just as poor as Guatemala pulled the plug on foreign adoption years ago, thereby preventing their children from enjoying those opportunities.

As more and more American would-be parents find they are unable to have children, or feel a calling, moral or religious, to reach into the "third world" and add to their families, as globalization and trade break down national borders, and as international adoption grows in popularity and as an industry, Americans have descended on Guatemala, not just for its coffee or fruit or textiles but for its children. (It is important to note that Europeans also adopted from Guatemala until their countries halted those programs because Guatemala was not Hague compliant. By mid-decade, adoption from Guatemala had become almost exclusively an American project.) According to the U.S. State Department, the number of Guatemalan children adopted annually by American families reached 4,727 in fiscal year 2007 after passing the 3,000 mark just four years earlier. Guatemala, a small country of approximately 13 million, passed Korea, Russia, and China in fiscal year 2008, to become the largest source of foreign adoption for the United States. In China's case, a one-child policy, coupled with a traditional feudal preference for male children, made thousands of baby girls expendable. Yet the number of Chinese adoptions by Americans was more than halved between 2005 and 2008, whereas adoptions from Guatemala rose by nearly 10 percent.

Guatemala, this magnificent land on the Central American isthmus of Mayan Indians, volcanoes, jungles, ancient temples and observatories, and a violent modern history, became the largest source for relinquishing its offspring in the entire world. In fact, a full 1 percent of all babies born in Guatemala during 2007 were adopted abroad.

Many American adoptive parents told me they were dissuaded from adopting within the United States when they heard horror stories, though often sensationalized, of the biological mother showing up three months later with a change of heart. Once they chose the international route, Guatemala appealed to many because of the reduced risk of the baby's having fetal alcohol syndrome, the incidence of which is much higher in eastern European countries than in Guatemala. And unlike China, where adoption is run by the state and babies are institutionalized, those parents adopting from Guatemala will not face the specter of walking into a crowded orphanage and picking a child out of several hundred. Guatemala's privatized notary distinction also flushed the system with money and led to top-rate, individualized care for children awaiting international adoption—a far cry from the packed orphanages in China.

Whereas a trip to Moscow, Beijing, or Seoul requires an exhausting journey through many time zones, Guatemala City is a short three-hour flight from Houston, Dallas, Miami, Atlanta, or Los Angeles, and many adopting parents also feel drawn there because of the notion that their child will retain his or her cultural roots and language on account of the proximity to a Spanish-speaking population in the United States. (The reality, however, is that most American middle-class and upper-middle-class families do not speak Spanish.)

Strictly in economic terms, at the height of international adoption, babies were not considered Guatemala's biggest export. The approximately twenty-five to thirty thousand dollars that an American family paid to adopt from there represented a hundred-million-dollar industry, though not one that would make or break Guatemala's gross domestic product. But in any suburban shopping mall in the United States, I would argue, it's not the *Hecho en Guatemala* ("Made in Guatemala") labels on packages of coffee or bananas or T-shirts that we consumers recognize: it's the sight of small brown-skinned children with deep-chocolate eyes being carried through the food court in the arms of their (usually) Caucasian parents. To many Americans, babies *seem* like Guatemala's greatest export. And almost every community in the United States has one now.

২৳

There was a good reason Americans were able to adopt more than four thousand kids a year from Guatemala and only a few hundred from the rest of Latin America combined. Critics called it simple *supply and demand*.

As much as 60 percent of the country's population is considered poor by international standards, and 30 percent are *extremely* poor. That means living on less than one dollar a day and usually going hungry. In Guatemala's rural Mayan Indian communities it means praying to the gods that the next corn harvest will be a good one; it means feeding watered-down coffee to babies in lieu of breast milk; it means traveling to faraway regions to find work, usually on the *finca* of some wealthy landowner; it means high infant mortality rates and little chance of a true education. In worst-case scenarios, boys sniff glue on the streets to quell their hunger or join gangs; girls sometimes resort to demeaning domestic work or prostitution. The Catholic and Evangelical churches rule the day there, and they all but forbid birth control. So the average Guatemalan woman has more than six children in her lifetime, some ten or even twenty, giving the lawyers who until recently controlled adoption an almost unlimited supply from which to choose.

The equally downtrodden populations of nearby Honduras, El Salvador, and Nicaragua are just as poor, of course, but their governments, and others all over the world, clamped down on the exodus of their flesh and blood when they signed the Hague Convention, which gives governments total control over adoptions within their borders. It is still possible to adopt from elsewhere in Central or South America, but the adopting parent is often required to live for months in that country to confront the bureaucratic system head-on, prove directly to that government that he or she is fit to raise the child, and ultimately learn Spanish, which most Americans adopting from Guatemala do not. Conversations with Guatemala's political elite and wealthy gave me the impression that they shy away from promoting foreign adoption en masse because they regard it as a national embarrassment when their most popular export is perceived to be their own children.

How did Guatemala become such a fertile market for foreign adoption? The country's lawyers were well aware of the rising demand in the United States for foreign babies, and they knew that their clients could pay upward of twenty to thirty thousand dollars per kid, sometimes more—an amount unimaginable to Guatemalan peasants. They also recognized that most Americans work full-time jobs and do not have the time to spend six months in Guatemala while the paperwork moved through the PGN, the Guatemalan equivalent of the attorney general's office. In the United States, time is money. So the objective of the lawyers was to make the process as quick and simple as possible for the adoptive parents: advertise photos of your cutest babies on the Internet; facilitate the process through e-mail; speak the language of your clients; don't make them wait any longer than they have to (because longing for your child is torture); and once they arrive in Guatemala City, hand them their baby in the lobby with enough instructions to get them through the next few days (or in some cases only a visit before the adoption is complete); escort them to the nearby American Embassy to finalize the child's visa; and, above all, make them feel welcome in their sheltered hotel community, one that isn't truly Guatemala.

That is not to imply that adoptive parents are willfully ignorant marionettes, blinded by a sense of entitlement, and herded by the attorneys from one exhibit to the next. Most of the adoptive parents I met were caring, intelligent, and pragmatic adults who recognized that they were experiencing an idealized, and sometimes fictionalized, Guatemala. Some even made the extra effort to know Guatemala, and their child's roots, by moving there for a year or more while waiting to complete the adoption process.

❧

What do Guatemalans think of international adoption? What do they think when they see gringos arriving in the capital by the planeload to stay a few days, visit the colorful indigenous markets by day, and drink piña coladas poolside by night before leaving with another one of their destitute children? Do they think the United States is draining Guatemala of its pure natural resources, like the coffee and fruit before it? Or are they grateful for the opportunities these kids will enjoy? The answer is, undoubtedly, both. I spoke to many Guatemalans who acknowledged the grinding poverty there and had few qualms with a system that would provide thousands of children with access to loving families with financial means. After all, the temptation of the American dream sends tens of thousands of Central Americans every year on the expensive and perilous journey with *coyote* human traffickers up through the Mexican desert and across the Rio Grande, dodging the watchful eyes of parasitic gangs and U.S. border guards, only to find backbreaking work in a society that often doesn't understand or respect them.

Babies adopted from Guatemala will never experience that treachery, because the moment their mother lays them down in a crib in their brand-new bedroom and sings a lullaby in English, their Americanization has begun. By the time they begin school, except for the color of their skin, their assimilation within the family will be well under way.

Guatemalan lawyers loved adoption, critics claim, because it was their livelihood. They made as much as twelve to fifteen thousand dollars per child, my sources told me, though some of that amount usually went to the intermediaries (adoption opponents sometimes used the term *jaladoras*, from *jalar*, or "to grab"), who sought out desperate pregnant mothers or, in some cases, recruited them to give up their children. Some money also went to notaries or anyone else who could make the adoption process more efficient. At times, the birth mothers were paid, too—as much as fifteen hundred dollars per child, claims UNICEF—though that is officially illegal because it violates the United Nations 1989 Convention on the Rights of a Child, which Guatemala signed. Key players on both sides of the adoption debate admitted to me that birth mothers' being paid, or given gifts, in exchange for their children was commonplace, though not necessarily true in all cases.

One respected Guatemalan adoption lawyer I spoke to did not see the handouts as gifts or payment, though. What changed hands was just a reimbursement for the costs incurred during the birth mother's nine-month pregnancy, he explained. Everything from food to housing and transportation costs for the Guatemalan woman's visits with the attorney in the capital contributed directly to the health of the babies, making the transactions legitimate. The number of lawyers working with adoption in Guatemala totaled only a few hundred at most, most of them full-time, though a handful practice other types of law and carried out an adoption transaction only when a desperate mother or intermediary approached them.

Because of corruption in the process, adoptions from Romania and other eastern European countries have been shut down, and elsewhere in Latin America they have slowed to a mere trickle as governments now control who can arrive and leave with their flesh and blood. The same fate now appears to have befallen Guatemala, whose congress passed the Ortega law in October 2007. That legislation essentially wrested control over foreign adoption away from the private-sector attorneys and the notary system and put it in the hands of the central government—all in accordance with the Hague Convention, which took effect in the United States in April 2008.

Since the end of fiscal year 2008, the number of new adoptions initiated by American families and approved by the State Department has essentially crashed to zero. Meanwhile, the Guatemalan government has gone back and reviewed hundreds of adoptions from 2006 and 2007 and, in some cases, heard claims from Guatemalan mothers that their babies were stolen. Women affiliated with the organization Fundación Sobrevivientes (Survivors Foundation) even staged a hunger strike in 2009 for three children who were allegedly stolen from their mothers' arms in 2006 and now live with families in the United States. If the window for Americans to continue adopting babies from Guatemala is to reopen, Washington has warned, Guatemala must completely reform its system.

Before the Guatemalan government ceased new adoptions in 2008, a precious few organizations within the country worked to shed light on the industry, that is, how the lawyers got the babies they eventually sold to American adoptive parents. UNICEF has spoken out in favor of the state's regulating adoption and encourages Guatemalans to adopt these children so they do not have to leave the country. But centuries of ugly racism and economic disparity have made this a nearly impossible goal. Not many Guatemalans can pay twenty-five thousand dollars for a child, and those with such money tend to be white, whereas the babies available for adoption are part- or full-blooded Mayan Indians—largely undesired by the upper class. Meanwhile, a nongovernmental organization named Casa Alianza has investigated and documented cases of babies being stolen from their mothers' arms or illegally put in orphanages under the pretense that their parents had abandoned them. In some instances the organization has actually returned babies to their homes before they could be adopted.

Yet those rare moral victories do not always mean practical solutions. An anecdotal story of a baby theft and recovery that I learned about in Quetzaltenango, in the western highlands, sums up this head-scratching dilemma. In 2005 foreign volunteers helped a birth mother find and legally reclaim the baby who had been stolen from her at the maternity ward and placed in a foster home and was on the verge of being adopted abroad. The happy reunion was short-lived, however. Within months of the return, the unsupervised baby was killed by an abusive older brother—a tragedy that might have been prevented had the child been adopted into a healthy home in the United States.

Death, whether accidental or intentional, seems to be everywhere in Guatemala. And both UNICEF and Casa Alianza understand the sad depths to which those who depend on the adoption industry will sink. The person who prepared a report on Guatemalan adoption for UNICEF in 2000 mysteriously disappeared a short time afterward, and one of Casa Alianza's investigative lawyers was gunned down by unknown assailants on his way to work in early September 2005—just days before I returned to Guatemala to write this book.

With the fate of attorney Harold Rafael Pérez Gallardo in mind, I reminded myself every day that extrajudicial killings are the norm in Guatemala, a country where there is no real law and order ("Why hire a lawyer when bullets are so cheap?" is a morbid local expression), and I needed to be careful whom I talked to and what questions I asked. This scarred country's brutal thirty-six-year civil war started largely as a result of post–World War II neocolonial U.S. influence and the CIA-executed coup d'état in 1954 and was most infamous for the Guatemalan death squads (trained and funded by the U.S. military) that wiped out entire indigenous villages in the 1980s. The United Nations–brokered Peace Accords were signed in 1996, but the violence never truly ended. The stakes only changed, and the fronts moved to urban areas, converting to gang violence and mafia-controlled trafficking of drugs . . . and people.

Of course, it is not just urban gangsters and human traffickers who have taken to violence over the subject of adoption. Villagers in a town near Lake Atitlán in 2006 tried to lynch a Guatemalan woman whom they accused of trafficking babies. And stories abound of foreigners venturing into rural villages and staring too long at a child or saying the wrong thing in broken Spanish to a frightened highland mother. Daniel Wilkinson reports in his book *Silence on the Mountain* that Mayan women wielding machetes attacked a foreigner during the waning days of the civil war for saying something like "Quiero tu hijo" ("I want your child," whereas she probably meant to say "I like your child"). The villagers probably heard the rumors that Guatemalan babies were being sold to foreigners to be chopped up for their organs. Wilkinson adds that the military may have spread these rumors in the highlands to scare the locals away from foreigners who were arriving in the 1980s and '90s to document the military massacres committed against the Mayan Indians. To this day, the belief that children are sold to the United States for their organs is widespread among rural Guatemalans, though there is no hard evidence to back it up, and not even UNICEF claims that the horrible rumor bears any legitimacy.

❧

As the most open and vocal critic of international adoption from Guatemala, UNICEF has come under an inferno of fire from adoption-advocacy groups, social workers, attorneys, and adoptive parents, both in Guatemala and in the United States. If you shut down the lifeline between impoverished Guatemala and families in the United States who are unable to have children, they claim, you deprive these kids of their inalienable right to a home, loving parents, food and nurture, and the support they need to thrive in life. These kids are not the *property* of Guatemala, adoption advocates like Hannah Wallace, executive director of Adoptions International, told me. If the state can't provide for them and guarantee that they will not die as infants or grow up to abuse, prostitution, and sniffing glue in city streets, then the state should welcome outside help.

Some in this camp even go so far as to call UNICEF an arrogant and self-serving organization that benefits from pictures of starving kids on the streets of a developing country like Guatemala. This is big business, UNICEF's bread and butter, more than one American adoption advocate told me, because every striking photo of a suffering child means more money for them.

Adoption advocates claim that the Guatemalan government may have proved a point and won a moral victory by eliminating attorney-controlled, privatized adoption, but the concrete result will be thousands of children stuck in poorly run state-controlled orphanages who would otherwise be on their way to homes in the United States. That is what has happened in other Latin American countries that have all but eliminated adoption, they say.

When I raised that point in 2006 with Guatemala's then first lady, Wendy de Berger, who pushed hard for adoption reform, she cast me an incredulous gaze and answered, "What thousands of kids? Show them to me. If there weren't an industry for our babies to be sold to American families," she added, "the lawyers wouldn't be paying women for their children. These kids aren't orphans. They had mothers, but those mothers were pressured to relinquish them."

During Berger's tenure as first lady, from 2004 to 2007, adoptive parents in the United States sent her photo albums of their children, originally from Guatemala and now seemingly happy and wealthy in the United States, as their way of lobbying her to keep the process open. But the first lady, who herself was educated in the United States, takes mild offense at the gesture. "I don't come to your country and tell you how to do things, so please don't come here and try to change our laws. . . . Adoption works very well in the United States. The problem is here in Guatemala. We have no control over our own children."

Berger's family, it must be pointed out, is among the well-to-do Guatemalan families that have adopted needy children—not Mayan Indian children from within their own country, ironically, but Caucasian children from eastern Europe. That fact has fueled the wrath that advocates of Guatemalan adoption feel toward Berger and UNICEF.

Despite the alleged anti-international adoption stances of UNICEF, Casa Alianza, the former first lady, and certain segments of the population, and despite the alleged unsavory practices of some adoption lawyers and their manipulation and bribing of uneducated poor women, all that is ominous about Guatemalan adoption would not overshadow the beautiful journey that is the backbone of this story, nor would it compromise the fairy tale that is life in a rich and developed country for a child who otherwise would have grown up virtually, if not literally, scavenging through a dump for food.

❧

When I set out to write a book on "the journey" of Guatemalan adoption in the summer of 2005, I hoped to tell the story from both ends. I wanted to capture the words of the poor, desperate birth mother who gives up her child, as well as those of the American family that embraces that same boy or girl and welcomes him or her into their home, opening up a whole new world of opportunity: airplane trips, iPods, high school proms, even a college education—unfathomable to anyone wandering the dirt paths of an impoverished Guatemalan village—but also identity crises, anger, and longing for their roots. In the spirit of the great odyssey, I also wanted to retell the events, both tragic and beautiful in their own right, of how these children lose a mother, a family, a home, everything they have known, and then how the doors of fortune miraculously open the day the child is whisked off to the United States.

Meanwhile, I hoped to go underground, dirty my hands if necessary, and investigate whether adoption is the murky and unsavory "industry" that many claim it is, without paying with my life in the process.

Finding a family in the United States who would volunteer to have their adopted child's past dug up was not going to be difficult, I discovered early on. The nearly twenty American families I interviewed over the summer of 2005 were eager to share every fleeting detail about their adopted children and what little they knew about the biological mothers, usually from the parts of the dossier translated into English. Americans love to brag about their kids, and why not? We are talking about beautiful wide-eyed tykes who, their parents believe, will grow up to be prom queens, valedictorians, and movie stars, all of them.

I settled on Judy Barrett and Bob Walters and their daughter Ellie as primary subjects because the girl had spent almost the first eight years of her life in Guatemala and was relinquished so late that she still remembered much of her past. Judy and Bob, like almost all adoptive parents I met, were open to the idea of their child meeting her biological mother someday, and that reflected how progressive the ideals of international adoption in the United States have become since the days when every trace of the child's former life was all but destroyed to protect him or her from the painful past.

But was the family ready to confront the demons that might rise to the surface if they unscrewed the cap and opened the bottle containing their little one's sad days in Guatemala: the hunger, the malnourishment, the domestic violence, the abuse, quite possibly the treatment of the baby as a commodity, and, worst of all, the abandonment? It would take a special kind of people to handle all this.

Judy and Bob in northern Michigan acknowledged the risks involved, yet they desperately wanted to find the mother who had given up their daughter, Ellie, seven years before—under circumstances that epitomize why adoption from Guatemala is so mysterious and so controversial.

PART I   *The Journey*

1 ❧ The Agony

The photo revealed an oblong wooden shack covered with shingles that had lost their white hue and succumbed to rot over the years as a result of torrents of rain pouring down from the metal sheet roof. Everything inside had undoubtedly gotten soaked, too. In the dirt yard in front of the building stood an old blue *pila* tub for washing clothes or bathing oneself, and a trail of water was visible between the cistern and the shack. Off to the left was a *jocote* tree that produced the sweet fruit common to this part of Central America. Scuff marks and carvings were visible on the tree's trunk and in its lower branches. Children must have played here: signs of life.

The house itself had two doorways, side by side: one was closed and looked boarded up, and the other was open and lacking a door or a window or anything to stop whatever or whomever from entering the premises. A closer look at the open doorway in the photo revealed only a pitch-black interior. Darkness.

It was a powerful and sobering photo, but it didn't tell half the story.

The neighbors could hear the sounds of panting and moaning coming from the open doorway, and if it wasn't the time of day when the noisy chicken buses passed through town and monopolized everyone's eardrums, the creaking of an old mattress in there, coming from the darkness, would have done it.

A matter of minutes after the noises began, sending the two boys playing in the *jocote* tree running away in disgust, the noises suddenly stopped, and out walked a peasant farmer, still buttoning up his trousers and looking around with caution to make sure no one was watching. Sweat dripped down his forehead and neck, soaking his tattered T-shirt, and his breath smelled like the rotgut *aguardiente* firewater he chugged to loosen up his morals before sleeping with the prostitute inside.

This is how it unfolded the five or six times she admits to doing it for money. It's certain that the neighbors knew, much of the village probably knew, and her own children definitely knew what she was doing in the darkness to earn enough money to put food in their little mouths. And for that, who can blame her? Like any good single mother, she was doing what was necessary to support her children.

For this was Tiquisate, a desolate poor town near Guatemala's southwestern coast, eight kilometers south of the Pacific highway, between Escuintla and Mazatenango. One main avenue ran through Tiquisate, and all the streets branching off of that were dirt paths littered with garbage where several thousand inhabitants made their homes in varying kinds of shanties.

Tiquisate existed because of the once booming sugarcane and banana industries that put the department of Escuintla on the map of the multinational corporation the United Fruit Company, which for decades exploited cheap labor and a never-ending supply of fresh fruit for its overseas profits. Before it abandoned Guatemala for more stable, and even cheaper, countries, the United Fruit Company made Tiquisate its southern base of operations and sent tons of bananas from the lowlands of Escuintla to the Caribbean port of Puerto Barrios on train tracks it owned.

A popular reformist president named Jacobo Arbenz tried to implement an agrarian reform policy in the early 1950s that would give peasants a share of the land on which they worked and tax foreign corporations on all the land they owned, not just the land they used. So the Boston-based United Fruit Company manipulated the red scare in the United States and convinced the Eisenhower administration to engineer a coup d'état in Guatemala in 1954, installing a brutal puppet dictator who clamped down on dissent. The seeds of civil war were sown, and the country's brutal conflict began six years later and wouldn't end until 1996.

So, of course, Tiquisate remained an important source for the fruit business. And like any industrial town, Tiquisate had plenty of jobs to offer locals as well as outsiders. The bananas needed to be harvested on the plantations, picked, and loaded into trucks, and the trucks needed to be serviced, maintained, and driven to the train tracks where the fruit would continue on to Puerto Barrios and the world beyond.

And wherever there was industry, there were prostitutes, often arriving from elsewhere to look for work. That's how a Salvadoran woman named Juana Antonia Cubillas Rodrigues escaped from her own impoverished war-torn country and arrived in Tiquisate sometime in the late 1980s.

❧

On a good day, six-year-old Eleanor Patricia Bereníce Ortiz Quipaz would have come home from her occasional job of picking up trash in the nearby market with as many as 10 quetzales (about $1.20) in her pocket. Bereníce, as they called her then, would have given her mother, Antonia, 9 of those quetzales to cover the cost of tortillas for the two of them and her three brothers—Maynor, William, and Erik—to eat. Antonia would have let her keep the final coin to buy a piece of candy.

But on a bad day Bereníce would have found her mother lying alone on a dirty mattress in the dark room, the sweat still glistening on her naked body and the unmistakable look of guilt filling her eyes like tears. Antonia's customer would have left a 20-quetzal bill and a cigarette butt on the dirt floor. The heavy air would have smelled like a mixture of cum, body odor, and liquor. And neither the mother on the soiled mattress nor the angry daughter in the doorway would have made a sound.

Bereníce knew what had happened. She was a perceptive kid. She heard the neighbors' gossip, she understood why Maynor and William ran away to play elsewhere in the village when a strange man came calling, and she couldn't forget that awful day when she and her brothers saw their mother in the river, completely naked, with another man, pushing themselves into each other like animals. Enraged, Bereníce threw rocks at her mother from the embankment to make her stop.

Her older brothers, on the other hand, had come to accept why Antonia did these things. By now they had probably even begun looking at girls themselves and felt a nervous sensation rising from the pits of their stomachs when they happened to make eye contact with one. They would have understood now that *sexo*—that act of a man with a crazed expression on his face pushing himself into a woman's musty private area—is both grotesque and beautiful at once. It was also necessary; it came as much from the stars as it did from that wretched bottle of firewater. And if men entering their mother and moaning in that god-awful manner would put food on the table, then so be it.

❧

Things weren't always this bad, Bereníce remembered. Before their father, Esvin, ran off with another woman named Esperanza and kicked them out of the house, there were happy times. Their papa worked as a mechanic, fixing the big trucks filled with bananas, and would sometimes let the boys, and even Bereníce, tag along and monkey with his tools. Or they'd run off and play in the mudflats next to the river outside of town. Bereníce never had any trouble keeping up with Maynor, William, and Erik. She learned to run as fast as they did, throw a ball as far as they could, and climb just as high in the *jocote* tree. They even went to school for a few years and began learning how to read and write Spanish.

Their papa made enough to support the family, though not a lot, and there were always tortillas on the table, sometimes even meat. Once or twice Antonia took the kids on long bus rides to El Salvador to visit her own mother, and Bereníce loved telling the other kids in Tiquisate how proud she was to be a *Salvadoreña*. For a time, the family was rich, though Bereníce had no idea where the money came from, and Antonia paid men to build a brand-new house out of concrete within sight of the main road that runs through Tiquisate. The house had several rooms, and there were a lot of trees nearby and even a hammock beside the front entrance, in which you could swing for hours.

Best of all, Bereníce's parents were together, a rarity in these parts.

But it all went awry once Esvin began drinking. He'd come home later and later in the evening and bark orders at the kids or at Antonia. He expected dinner to arrive on his plate the very moment he walked in the door, he stopped taking any interest in his sons or daughter, and neighbors would see him around town sporting with another woman. And when he learned that Antonia was pregnant again, by him no doubt, he began to hit her, claiming the child to come wasn't his, and accusing her of running around with other men.

She wasn't, though. That would come later.

Then came the day when Esvin arrived with Esperanza, his girl-friend, and said that while the baby in Antonia's belly *wasn't* his responsibility, the house *was* his, saying he had built it, which he had not, and ordering Antonia and the kids to leave. Maynor, William, and Erik cried because they couldn't understand why their father was acting this way, but Esperanza—the woman whom Bereníce remembers as stealing their daddy— would have none of it. She told Esvin to beat the boys if they wouldn't obey, and after that to deny that he was their father.

Esperanza (whose name ironically translates as "hope") was his new woman, Esvin said, and there wasn't room in the house for Antonia or the kids. They had to go. And their mama had to find other means to support their family. In Guatemala's lawless, machismo culture, men can get away with treating women like this. There are no women's resource centers, no child-support laws, nothing.

Sometime after that, but before the longing in Antonia's heart had left her completely, she invited witchcraft into their house. The children came home from the market to the gray shack near the *jocote* tree and found their mother on her knees in the dark room, placing candles around the dirt floor. The strange women in the village often dismissed as *brujas*, or witches, had brought them, and Antonia might have thought they could help exorcise the demons that Esvin had released upon their family, although that's not clear. Antonia had never been a religious woman, and if what happened next was to have any symbolic significance, it was probably the *brujas* in Tiquisate who planted the idea in her head.

Antonia gathered Maynor, William, Berenice, and Erik in the room and asked them to close the door and step carefully to avoid kicking over the candles, which she lit one by one. Then Berenice remembers their mother producing a wooden bowl and asking each member of the family to urinate in it. The kids probably would have thought the act to be strange, and even a little demented, but to this day they are all sensitive to the feelings of others. They would have known how much pain their mother was in from losing Esvin, so they would have obeyed. And then, Berenice remembers, Antonia passed around the wooden bowl filled with urine, and asked each member of her family to take a drink.

Was this a ceremonial way to pull the family back together? Was it an old Salvadoran tradition? Berenice is the only one who remembers this strange afternoon, and she can't explain why it happened.

Finally, Antonia pulled out the thickest, darkest cigarette they had ever seen (likely a cigar, though they are not common in Guatemala), lit it with the help of a candle, and encouraged each child to suck on the end that wasn't burning.

They rarely talked about their father again after that.

❧

"*Hola, amiga*, how are those kids of yours doing? Are they getting enough to eat?" Antonia heard a voice directed at her from behind a stack of fresh tortillas wrapped in a giant red woven cloth to keep them warm. The delicious smell captured her attention, but the voice was familiar, too.

Lately, a woman named Estela, who worked in the market and provided families in Tiquisate with their staple food, had begun asking Antonia more and more often about her children. Not that that was strange. In Latin America, cordially engaging in small talk with each person you meet on a daily basis is common practice. Tiquisate itself was small, and nearly everyone knew each other. And it was no secret that Antonia had lost children to malnutrition, or at least that's what the villagers had been told. Erik, the younger brother of Maynor, William, and Berenice, was a pale and sickly looking boy who couldn't gain weight no matter how many tortillas he shoveled into his mouth. No one had seen him in months, so the assumption was that he had died, at four years old, though there was never a funeral procession, and he had no grave in the Tiquisate cemetery. Death was an everyday occurrence here, and you didn't question it or mourn over it too long because there were always more hungry mouths to feed. And so the question of what really happened to Erik had been forgotten.

Still, at the tortilla stand in the bowels of the crowded market, Estela's questions reached deeper than a superficial level, and Antonia wondered why she wanted to know so much.

"That daughter of yours—Berenice. She's a pretty little thing. Does she cry?"

Sometimes Antonia found the woman's voice condescending and her questions suspicious. But she was much too shy to protest, so when Estela asked if she could come and visit the family in their home, "together with a very wise friend of mine from out of town," Antonia didn't dare say no. After all, the mother might have been thinking, this woman has her own tortilla shop in the market, so she must be smarter than I am. Maybe she even had work to offer Berenice?

For a time Estela's voice became as familiar to the children's ears as the pat-pat of Antonia clapping a dough of maize into tortillas every morning. The woman's visits usually took place after breakfast, once the thin corn-based patties had been eaten with beans and sometimes rice, the floor of the shack had been swept, and the older boys were off climbing the *jocote* tree or playing soccer in the village. Antonia's customers never arrived until the afternoon, so late morning was the perfect time for Estela to pay a visit and conduct business.

It all began innocently enough, Estela arriving to greet Antonia and sometimes bringing a little gift for Beneníce, like a piece of candy or a hair ribbon. She was becoming a friend of the family, this strange woman from the market. So why question her kindness? Estela made Beneníce laugh as a young girl should. And what was so wrong with asking Antonia about her job, about her finances, about the children's health, about whether they were happy, about whether they would like to go on a trip with Estela?

When Estela's friend Doña Cesy arrived from a region near the Mexican border called Tecún Aman and began not asking but *telling* Antonia that she was dirt poor, that her work was despicable and evil, that her kids were malnourished and small, and that the little girl would have a better life elsewhere, Antonia became worried. She knew something was up, and she wished she could stop it from happening. But all her life she had felt subordinate to people around her: people with conviction or physical power, people who spoke in firm voices and looked her directly in the eye, people who were educated, people who had better jobs than she, and people who must have had a better idea than she did of what course to take.

Esvin took her house and made her leave with the kids. Before him, the same thing had happened with another man in El Salvador who fathered three of her children, before Maynor was born. The men who slept with her now for money dictated when they'd show up and how much time they would spend with her on the mattress. More recently, Estela had entered her life and talked to Beneníce about going on trips to see other, richer, parts of Guatemala. Antonia wished she could gain control over things, but how?

To make matters worse, with Beneníce, Doña Cesy was an instant hit. She told the curious girl about the area of the country she came from, where the mountains towered into the sky and where the rivers flowed fast: where the indigenous people still wore colorful, hand-woven clothing and spoke in funny languages. She told Beneníce about the places they could travel together: the capital city with its big roads, tall buildings, and people everywhere. People there aren't poor like they are in Tiquisate, Doña Cesy lied. They always have enough to eat, and they don't lose younger siblings at childbirth as Berenice had . . . or so she was told.

The world out there was new and exciting.

Cesy didn't spend so much time discussing these things with Antonia, and when she did, she talked down to the mother, occasionally barking out orders. "Get me a plate of food," she might have said. And with each visit, Antonia felt herself losing more and more control over the future. When the women left, and the house turned quiet again, Berenice often asked her mother, "When can we travel, Mama? When can we go to Guatemala City?" And, of course, Antonia had no answer for that, because taking her girl away from Tiquisate was never her idea.

In her own home, Antonia felt powerless over the fate of her children.

2 ❧ "Why Can't We?"

This wasn't the first time Judy Barrett had seriously considered adopting a child. Back in her wild twenties, when she wasn't afraid to backpack around South America, and when she figured she could save the world just by speaking up, Judy considered going into social work, and her most immediate contribution to setting the world straight would be to bring one of those poor motherless Ecuadorian *Quichua* children she saw chewing coca leaves on the streets of Quito back to the Midwest and raise the little girl herself. But then she talked to a social worker friend and had to sit through one horror story after another until she was convinced that raising someone else's impoverished kid was not going to be all fun and glory.

Not long after that, her twins, Amelia and Elizabeth, entered the picture, and their father left town before he even got a chance to meet them. Judy's hands were full raising her daughters, and she completely forgot about foreign adoption.

The girls were five years old when Judy married Bob Walters, a tall and gentle man whose work with the forestry service in northern Michigan fitted well his patient and straightforward demeanor. Bob was a good man, a dependable oak, and with him Judy could completely close the chapter on the twins' father, who never returned.

That man, with whom she had a brief affair that never would have happened had she not fallen for his mysterious, nomadic ways, left when he learned she was pregnant, and he never even made an effort to meet his daughters. Judy hired a lawyer to find the phantom father in case his consent was needed for Bob to officially adopt the twins.

But the search turned up nothing. The man had disappeared from the face of the earth, making Bob their new father. He adopted Amelia and Elizabeth. But then, it wasn't really adoption because, as Bob said, "they came with the package . . . with Judy."

The five-year-old twins accepted Bob as their new father without reservation. The night before the wedding, all they could think about was how this was a great opportunity to wear party dresses.

Judy's own mother had been adopted domestically—she knew that. And Judy figured out on her own that her mother's biological mom had left her on a doorstep. Throughout her youth, going away on any trip was always a pain because Judy's mother acted as if she were being abandoned one more time. But her family never talked much about the abandonment. She grew up in a blue-collar home in Detroit in the 1950s with the only income coming from her father's work on the automobile assembly line. Whatever therapy existed at the time would have been expensive, and healing her mother's emotional wounds wasn't going to put food on the table. Judy's mother was buried five years ago with a diseased liver from drinking away the pain of her abandonment.

So it wasn't until the girls came home from school one day, raving about their friends, the Grettenbergers, and their five adopted kids, that the subject reentered Judy's mind. "Why can't we adopt?" Amelia and Elizabeth asked. "Why can't we have a little sister from a foreign country?" Instead of dismissing the request as the silly wishes of pre-teenagers, Judy called up the Grettenbergers. She already knew them and had held them in high regard because Lou and Karen Grettenberger headed a Methodist congregation in their hometown of Traverse City, Michigan, and, like Judy, identified as being politically liberal.

"They live a mile away, and they are our best friends," Judy told Bob. "Like us, they are a musical family. And they love third world problems. Their Russian son has clubfeet, and another is missing an arm. They don't know what they're getting, and they don't care. How come Karen is doing that and I'm not?"

And so the wheels began spinning. Judy's brother was traveling to

Hong Kong on a business trip to look at machine tools, and he invited her to join him. She checked out the Pearl River piano plant and, while she was in the neighborhood, visited an orphanage for mostly handicapped children, many of whom would end up being adopted by American families, some even by fellow guests at the hotel where they were staying.

China is the first country many Americans consider when they decide to adopt from a foreign country. Since the emerging empire opened its borders in the late 1980s, it has signed off on the rights to more than seven thousand children a year, mostly because the Chinese government promotes a one-child policy in an effort to limit its population growth and industrialize itself. The result of that one-child policy has been women abandoning their extra children, mostly girls because they are not valued as highly as boys, on city streets, in public parks, and on the doorsteps of orphanages, knowing they will be cared for and adopted abroad.

But the influx of abandoned babies, and the Chinese government's policy of controlling adoption, has institutionalized the system and filled orphanages to the brim, sometimes with hundreds of children. When adopting parents walk through these baby wards, they often feel overwhelmed by the cries of abandoned tykes and, ultimately, turned off by Chinese adoption. Judy Barrett had this reaction, though for a different reason. To her, the adoption process here seemed complicated and inefficient. She wasn't allowed to see much at the orphanage, and the kids were kept at arm's length. Plus, China just seemed so far away. And far away was not a place that appealed to Bob.

Bob was the quieter of the two, the rock in the relationship, while Judy was the go-getting entrepreneur. She ran the successful Traverse City outlet of Wild Birds Unlimited, a nature store in the middle of town that sold everything from bird feeders to binoculars. Bob's career, on the other hand, was embedded in a deep, solitary love for Michigan's old growth forests. He would rather spend a day wandering through the whispering pine trees that cover the northern half of the state than he would schmoozing with customers looking for souvenirs before they headed back down to urban southern Michigan to their jobs and lives.

And so, like many big decisions the couple had entertained since they married six years before, it was Judy who was receptive almost immediately to the twins' wild suggestion that they adopt a child and Bob who mulled over the suggestion for days, debating each factor and possible outcome, just as he would have done before authorizing the removal of a giant tree whose branches interfered with the widening of a country road. Judy thought back to her younger days when she traveled, and even lived for a time, in Latin America. She still spoke rudimentary Spanish, and once she had convinced Bob that they could pull this off, and once they had ruled out China, it wasn't long before Judy and Bob began looking south.

With Guatemala already in mind, Judy went online and began e-mailing orphanages, inquiring about an older girl who might be available. Judy and Bob didn't want to raise an infant, that was clear, but they also didn't want someone older than Amelia and Elizabeth who would alter the sibling pattern.

It wouldn't take long before Judy got her reply.

3 ❧ The Relinquishment

"Mañana, vamos a la capital." Tomorrow we go to the capital. The words leaving Antonia's mouth seemed almost forced, as if a cruel captor were standing over her, beating her back with a stick until she made that fateful pronouncement to her nearly eight-year-old daughter. So now, after months of painful deliberation and nagging guilt trips from Estela, the woman in the market who sold tortillas, and Doña Cesy, her mysterious friend from Tecún Aman, Antonia pronounced those five words, and in doing so decided to give Bereníce up for adoption. Tomorrow we go to the capital.

But the girl didn't know the reason for this impromptu trip to Guate, which is how the locals refer to Guatemala City. She was told that they would visit an aunt in the capital whom neither she nor her brothers Maynor or William had ever heard of before.

Did Antonia feel guilty about lying to her daughter about what was to come? Perhaps. At least she told the two boys the real reason for the trip, so that they could enjoy their last forty-eight hours with their sister. And they were to keep their lips tightly sealed.

Aunt or no aunt, the afternoon before their departure Bereníce felt giddier than she ever had before. The family hadn't been on a trip together since the days when their father, Esvin, was still around and they had enough money to visit Antonia's mother in El Salvador on occasion. But even then they never spent any time in the capital city. Guate was always a point of transit for San Salvador.

For months now Cesy had been tempting Bereníce with stories of big-city glamour whenever she visited Tiquisate. There was Tikal

Futura, the elegant multistory mall in the heart of downtown with arcades, cinemas, and a five-star hotel. The name Tikal Futura suggested that the architects were trying to build a successor to the magnificent Mayan ruins at Tikal in northern Guatemala. There was Zona 10, the richest part of the capital, where the tree-lined boulevards, nightclubs, and fancy cars resembled Miami more than they did a developing country. And of course, there was noise and people everywhere. It would be nothing like Tiquisate, Cesy promised.

Since they would leave before dawn, Berenice was told to retire early and get a good night's sleep. The trip on the bus the next day would be long and arduous, and she would enjoy it more if she were well rested. But sleep? Honestly, how could she fall asleep when such an exciting day awaited her? Berenice could only lie awake all night, pestering anyone who would listen, in anticipation of the next day's events.

She had no idea what awaited her at the other end of her journey.

꙰

Relinquishment and foreign adoption were certainly unusual for someone as old as Berenice. Most of the thousands of Guatemalan children who are adopted into the United States every year come as infants less than a year old so their new parents can experience them as babies and give them a fresh start, a rebirth, nearly free of the "separation anxiety" and painful memories that Americans automatically associate with third world Guatemala. Berenice, on the other hand, was almost eight years old, and the relationships she had formed with her mother, her brothers, and the village around her would be part of her forever. To remove her at this point from everything she knew and loved was an act a thousand times more sinister than taking a newborn from its crib after only a few days of life.

Her story is a prime example of why adoption is considered so controversial in Guatemala. Foreign adoption has traditionally been reserved for orphans deprived of their birth mothers through wars and other disasters. But as all characters in this story attest, Berenice's mother and brothers were very much alive and part of her life. True, they were extremely poor and forced into degrading work like prostitution and sweeping market floors, and she and her brothers had already dropped out of school since there was no money for such things, but outside players coming into the home and convincing Antonia to relinquish the already seven-year-old girl certainly raised moral questions.

UNICEF supports international adoption only as a last resort, once the options of extended family and adoption within the country of origin are exhausted, and for its stance it has drawn the fiery wrath of Guatemalan adoption advocates in the United States for depriving kids of homes in *El Norte*. UNICEF calls women like Doña Cesy and Estela *jaladoras*, from the Spanish verb *jalar*, to grab. Others refer to them as *coyotes*, in reference to the sly nocturnal animals and the human traffickers who lead Latin American immigrants on the perilous journey up through Mexico to smuggle them into the United States. But these women call themselves *intermediarias*, intermediaries, or *cuidadoras*, the term traditionally reserved for the sweet old grandmotherly foster mothers in Guatemala City or Antigua who care for the babies while the American adoptive parents wait for the legal process to run its course.

The *jaladoras* can range from women who work in the local market, like Estela who knows which women in the village have a surplus of kids, to nurses or midwives in a hospital who have firsthand access to women giving birth to children they might have trouble caring for, to someone like Cesy who will show up in the impoverished household with gifts to woo a mother, or a child. Almost anyone can be a *jaladora*, anyone who has contact with the lawyers in Guatemala City who facilitate international adoption. And not all of them are manipulative and self-serving like those who convinced Antonia to relinquish Berenice. Many simply know pregnant women who don't want to have another child and frown upon, or don't have access to, abortion, and they offer to help by placing a call to a confidant in the capital.

That's what happened in the case of a woman I met named Doña Gloria, a middle-class woman in Coatepeque, in Guatemala's western coffee-producing region near the Mexican border. Gloria became a *cuidadora* when she learned through a mutual friend about Norma, an impoverished mother of two teenagers who had accidentally become pregnant through a secret affair. Norma, who earned a meager three dollars a day picking coffee beans, decided not to tell her children or her seventy-year-old father, Sabino, who also lived with them in a nearby village. Gloria read in the national newspaper, the *Prensa Libre*, that Guatemala was a popular source of adoption for American couples. She had also read about newborn babies in Coatepeque being found in trash dumps or attacked by wild dogs, literally left out to die by poor desperate mothers who didn't know what to do with them. Though she hadn't done this before, Gloria invited Norma into her comfortable home where together they would hide the secret.

The two women found a newspaper advertisement for expectant mothers in distress and called a lawyer in Guatemala City to facilitate the relinquishment once the child was born. But first Gloria made sure that Norma was ready to give up her child: "If you can raise the baby well, then you should keep it. But if not, give it up." Gloria loaned Norma money for the rent, medicine, and food during the second and third trimesters, knowing that the attorney would reimburse her for those costs. But the birth mother would not be paid for her child. Gloria was no *jaladora*, and this was about finding a good home for the infant, not about making a profit. Less than two weeks after the birth, Norma brought the little girl to Guatemala City and gave it to her foster parents. She now lives in Tennessee with the Hayman family, who call her McKenna.

All adopting parents want to believe that the journey of their little one mirrors that of McKenna more than it does that of Berenice, who was coerced out of Antonia's hands for the profit of those Guatemalans who facilitate international adoption.

❧

"¡Guate, Guate!" The ticket collector leaned out the passenger door of the old yellow school bus and yelled out the destination for any passengers perusing the Tiquisate market who had yet to jump on board. This was the 5:00 a.m. bus that would head east on the Pacific highway toward Escuintla, and then north toward the capital, arriving in Guatemala City at around 7:30. Just in front of it was another "chicken bus" pulling out of the market area and onto Tiquisate's main drag, this one heading west for Mazatenango. The first bus spat out a cloud of dark, stinky diesel fumes that surrounded the Guate-bound ticket collector like a wreath, and to the market vendors unwrapping their wares nearby, it might have looked as if he were disappearing into the puff of smoke.

"¡Guate, Guate!" he yelled again between coughs. And at the driver's request he retreated into the bus to collect fares. The folding door shut, and the old yellow school bus that still bore "School District Teaneck, New Jersey" above the driver's rearview mirror pulled away from Tiquisate. On it, and all crammed into one seat together, were Antonia, Maynor, and William. Doña Cesy and the girl, Eleanor Patricia Bereníce Ortiz Quipaz, would follow them on the 6:00 a.m. bus, so as not to tip off anyone else in the village to the purpose of this life-changing journey. This was Cesy's idea. She knew how people in Tiquisate felt about adoption. She had heard the rumors that babies from third world countries were being adopted for their body parts, and she knew it was a lie. But scary folklore always catches on among the poor and isolated, and she wanted Antonia to proceed with discretion.

"When you return here, tell anyone who asks that the girl died, or that she's back in El Salvador with your mother. Don't mention adoption," Cesy advised Antonia, who at that very moment, as the bus headed north toward the highway and Tiquisate gave way to fields of sugarcane, was entering her own personal hell. She already missed her daughter terribly, even though she would see Bereníce in a few hours in Guatemala City, but she knew she was about to lose her. And she knew it was her own fault. Again, her inability to act, to stand up for herself: that awful weakness that had plagued her throughout her poverty-stricken thirty-four years on this earth.

Betty Jean Lifton, the author and well-respected adoption counselor, captured a universal truth about the way birth mothers are casually asked to forget about their babies once they are given up for adoption. "So, too, the birth mother, from the moment she surrenders her baby, is forced into this double life. Advised by the 'experts' to pretend it never happened, she never tells anyone what was probably the most important and traumatic event of her life . . . her baby, gone, in a relinquishment as irrevocable as death." Though Lifton wrote these words years before the flood of adoptions from Guatemala began, she might as well have been analyzing Cesy's advice to Antonia.

"I can still stop this from happening," a voice in Antonia's head sounded the alarm. "Their bus doesn't leave for another forty-five minutes. The boys and I can jump off right now and walk back to town, and meet them at the market."

"But you've already promised Doña Cesy and Estela that you'd go through with this," another voice countered. "You can't back down now. They'll be angry."

"But this is my girl, Bereníce! They can't take her away from me without my permission."

"You've already given her up. It's too late. Everyone is counting on you. The people waiting in Guatemala City are counting on you."

"But what if Bereníce doesn't want to leave me? She thinks we're only going to visit an aunt. I lied to her."

"Bereníce *does* want to go. She wants to go see the big city and visit all the sights that Doña Cesy described to her. Didn't you see her last night? She couldn't wait to travel."

"But Doña Cesy is evil. She's only manipulating us so she can have my girl."

"Doña Cesy is not evil. She's a good woman. And she's much smarter than you are. She has a good job; she has money; she is sophisticated and has friends in other countries. She knows more about what's best for the girl than you do. You're just a poor, stupid whore. You let people walk all over you, both men and women."

Though Maynor and William lay sound asleep next to her, Antonia felt tormented, the voices in her head arguing back and forth, creating tremors from her head down to her heart. And of course, the bus was nearing Escuintla, which meant they were almost halfway there. It was far too late to turn back.

She slumped into her seat, feeling defeated again. This time it wasn't just men crawling between her legs and using her for sex, or women overcharging her for fruit in the market. This time it was about her daughter, her own daughter. This time it was forever.

᛫

Bereníce had hardly slept during the night, yet when Estela nudged her and told her it was time to walk to the terminal for the second bus to the capital, she jumped up, as wide awake and alert as a child on Christmas morning. This was the big day, she told herself. They were going to Guate!

Doña Cesy was waiting for them at the market, and she had probably already purchased provisions for the journey: fruit, tortillas, and bottles of water. They got onto the 6:00 a.m. yellow school bus to Guatemala City, which would already have been filling up, because this was midmorning by rural Central American standards. Remember, Antonia and the boys had taken the first bus to avoid arousing suspicion among the townspeople that she was giving up her child.

In the Guatemalan "chicken bus," the passengers crowded three or four to a seat that was actually intended for no more than two American schoolchildren. Luckily, most of these people were small in stature. Those who arrived late, or hailed the bus to stop after it had left the Tiquisate market, would have to stand hip to hip in the aisle for the whole journey, for fellow passengers had packed everything imaginable onto the bus with them. In the overhead compartment was a cardboard box with live chickens in it (hence the name "chicken bus"). A woman seated behind our party carried a large bucket in her lap with delicious corn tamales inside under a cloth, which she would sell during the bus ride. A man opened the emergency door in the back and beckoned the people in the aisle to hop up, one by one, as he slid a stack of two-by-four boards up the aisle.

At five minutes to six, the driver cranked the radio and blared Latino dance music through the broken speakers, finding every ear in the bus. That was the signal for the vendors to hawk their wares before departure. On stepped a little girl no older than Berenice, who shimmied around the bodies standing in the aisle, selling Chiclets to anyone interested. But here, nearly everyone was poor, and the response to the Chiclets was lukewarm at best.

Following her there appeared a grisly looking man standing next to the driver's seat and missing his right arm. He faced the passengers and began reciting a biblical sermon about helping the poor, all the while holding up the good book with his left arm, the one he hadn't lost in an unfortunate machete accident in the sugarcane fields. Guatemalans were used to these everyday scenes and thought nothing of them. But anyone trying to ignore the spectacle of the loud, handicapped preacher and catch a snooze found himself hard-pressed to look away when his sermon approached a climax and he took off his shirt to reveal the grotesque stump where his right arm had been until, apparently, fairly recently.

Of course, this was the kind of dangerous and demeaning work in the fields that awaited Maynor and William when they got a little older and strong enough to swing a machete hundreds of times a day.

His speech finished, the one-armed man walked through the bus passing out candy bonbons to anyone who would hand over a few quetzales "in the name of God" but also to help him buy his daily bread. Then he exited the bus, the driver took his seat, the doors closed, and Berenice, still giddy with anticipation, watched Tiquisate disappear out the window, not knowing that years would pass before she returned.

Berenice didn't notice it because her thoughts were elsewhere, but the landscape all around her, as the bus turned east on the Pacific highway toward Escuintla, was absolutely breathtaking. The coastal lowlands rolling by offered sugarcane fields as far as the eye could see, as well as pineapple orchards, banana trees, and other ripe fruits that would make sun-starved North Americans drool at the mere notion. This was July 1999, and the rainy season had just begun, so the landscape was lush and green. Here and there were cattle ranches, usually owned by wealthy Spaniards, some of whom were rumored to use their livestock and land as a front for smuggling Colombian cocaine into the United States.

Oh, but look to the north and there were Guatemala's famous volcanoes. A white cloud of fumes seeped out of Volcán de Atitlán, at the southern base of Lago de Atitlán, the most beautiful lake in the world. The chain continued eastward, these amazing natural landmarks that appear on every Guatemalan tourist brochure and hand-woven Mayan place mat. To many tourists, these volcanoes overshadow the grinding poverty here.

But for the people who see them every day, they go unnoticed—natural giants on the horizon. When the bus turned north toward Guatemala City, it passed by Volcán de Pacaya, an active beast spitting out smoke almost every evening. Now they were climbing toward a higher elevation, a different ecosystem and a different culture altogether. Berenice and Cesy felt their ears pop. As they left the lowlands, they even put on sweaters.

❧

The bus terminal in Guatemala City was not the kind of place you wanted to be without a purpose, a destination, and a reliable contact to help you get there, not even at eight thirty in the morning. Gangs and armed robbers owned these streets, and they faced little competition from the police or from the military. Guatemala's civil war had officially ended only two and a half years previously, in December 1996, and one of the United Nations' key stipulations was that the military disarm and go home. A power vacuum ensued, creating a fertile breeding ground for the rival pan–Central American gangs Mara Salvatrucha and 18 to kill each other, over and over again.

The tattooed bad boys could tell which people were local, which were foreign, who were their own, and whom to kill. And Antonia,

Maynor, William, Bereníce, and Cesy—once they reunited at the bus terminal—stuck out in this urban environment because they were still wearing their shorts and T-shirts. They were definitely unable to conceal their coastal dialects. So, as the point person for this adoption trip, it was Cesy's job to get them out of there as quickly as possible. She found a pay phone near the terminal, and called Cassandra, the head of the orphanage, who told her to hop on another bus for Antigua, a tourist town forty-five minutes away and, culturally, a world away from Guatemala City.

To get from the capital to Antigua, where foreign backpackers came to take Spanish classes and where the upper-class Guatemalans came to get drunk and pick up gringas, you drove west, up into the mountains and then down into a beautiful valley where Antigua sat, nestled between Volcán de Agua to the south and the Cero de la Cruz, the hill of the cross to the north. Antigua was the Guatemalan capital until an earthquake wiped it out in 1773. But it was still the playground of the rich, which was why many of the lawyers and orphanage directors who facilitate international adoption used Antigua, or one of the wealthy hotels in Guatemala City like the Marriott, as their base of operations.

It was chilly up in the mountains between Guate and Antigua, and Bereníce realized quickly that she was in a whole new world. On the roadsides around her highland Mayan Indian women dressed in their colorful *trajes* hawked their embroidered wares. And fast sports cars with tinted black windows flew by the bus in the left-hand lane. These were the rich kids from the capital, and they preferred tinted windows so that potential thieves couldn't see the toys they had inside their cars: expensive stereo systems, Armani suits, laptop computers.

But the culture shock hit her a second time when they pulled into Antigua's bus terminal, disembarked, and walked through the crowded market and out onto the main thoroughfare, where she saw the gringos right away: either the true budget backpackers waiting for chicken buses to take them west to Lake Atitlán, with five o'clock shadows on their faces and Nalgene water bottles attached to their packs, and even the three-star-hotel tourists taking a break from their jobs back home to study Spanish for a couple of weeks. The fat-pocket businessmen or American couples coming here to adopt avoided the chaotic market and bus terminal, sticking instead to comfortable shuttle busses to transport them to and fro.

Bereníce remembered seeing gringos only once before this, and that was back home in Tiquisate. The two tall, pale visitors were walking down the main street, and at the sight of them she had run home in fright to tell her mother. They were probably missionaries of some sort, because foreign tourists were unheard of in Tiquisate.

By ten thirty in the morning on what the records indicate to be July 20, 1999, Cesy had checked the group of five into an inexpensive hotel, with Cesy in one room and the family sharing the other, near the market. Since they were exhausted from the long journey, the party took a good long nap. This was why Bereníce falsely remembered arriving in Antigua at night, because she was exhausted and because they slept soon afterward.

July is the rainy season in Guatemala, and the sky opened up around two in the afternoon and rained torrents for an hour or two, creating a rhythmic pitter-patter on the hotel's sheet-metal roof and giving the plants in the open-air courtyard a healthy dose of water. The sound of the rain wasn't soothing to Antonia—part of her already regretted what she was doing, but she didn't have the courage not to go through with it. She was unable to sleep through the rain.

Later on, the party of five left the hotel and ventured out for dinner. Doña Cesy treated. She was the only one who had any money, and she felt some sense of responsibility for helping the family, given that she knew what was going to happen in the morning. They ate at a hole-in-the-wall restaurant on the main street, about two blocks north of the market, called Pupusería Sapo y la Rana, where a toad and a frog are painted on the wall above the entrance, locked in a happy embrace. This restaurant specializes in *pupusas*, delicious fried-cheese pancakes that are best when filled with hot sauce and coleslaw. *Pupusas* can be found in Guatemala, but they are even more popular in El Salvador, Antonia's homeland.

By the end of the meal, Bereníce was full of questions, as any curious seven year old would be. "Where did all these gringos come from? Why are the streets so clean here? When are we going to visit our aunt? What will we do here tomorrow?"

Antonia, stone-faced, staring at the wall, didn't know what to say. "¿Saber?" was her curt answer. Who knows? said in a tone of hopeless despair.

And this was Cesy's cue to jump in and tell a lie. She had been cheerful and talkative the whole journey, and Bereníce couldn't figure out why this friend of the family was so happy while her mother was so depressed. "Tomorrow we'll visit the beautiful Parque Central, just four blocks away, where the gringos play guitar and sing in funny languages near the fountain with a stone statue of a beautiful woman. We'll eat *hamburguesas* like they do in *El Norte*, and we'll climb the hill of the cross and look out over all of Antigua."

Bereníce smiled. And once again, she wouldn't be able to fall asleep at night, out of sheer anticipation of what was to come.

❦

"You stay here," is what Maynor and William remembered Doña Cesy telling them the next morning. "We have some important business to take care of, and we'll be back in a couple hours."

Of course, the boys already knew what was about to take place today, and there was no way they were going to let their sister go without a fight. Bereníce remembered Cesy locking the door of the room when they and Antonia left the hotel, but somehow the boys escaped. And when the women and the girl arrived at the office of Cassandra Elizabeth Gonzalez Arriba, who, along with her American husband, Clayton Phelpers, ran an orphanage named Hogar Nuevo Día outside of Antigua, Maynor and William were sneaking along behind them.

The outside of the building where Cassandra worked was nondescript, since many involved in Guatemalan adoption seek to maintain a low profile. But once Cesy, Antonia, and Bereníce entered the office, they saw the words *Hogar Nuevo Día, para Niños* written on a sign on the wall and on stationery on a desk. *Hogar* is the politically correct term in Guatemala for an orphanage because it doesn't suggest poor street kids begging for more gruel in a Charles Dickens novel. *Hogar* simply means "home." Furthermore, not all kids living in a *hogar* are orphans. Many have just been abandoned, or, better put, "relinquished," by their birth mothers. That would soon be the case with Berenice.

The door to the office locked, Maynor and William found a window and peeked inside, rubbing their noses against the glass and trying to poke their heads in to see more. They were curious, like any boys of nine and ten. But they didn't find Berenice or Antonia. They saw Cassandra, who scowled when she caught two little boys spying through her office window. She walked toward the window and gave them an angry look. The boys ran away in fright. "I would never accept those rowdy little rascals in my *hogar*," she would tell a confidante later on.

Meanwhile, in the reception area, the critical moment was almost at hand. "What are we doing here?" Berenice asked her mother.

"You'll see," Antonia managed to say, though it was difficult for her to speak.

Cassandra entered the room and, like Cesy before her, inevitably said something sweet and comforting to the girl who was about to pass into her care. She beckoned the party into her office, and everyone sat down in chairs. Cassandra, Cesy, and Antonia carried on a conversation about things that Berenice didn't understand, which lasted no more than twenty minutes. Because of Cesy's numerous visits to Tiquisate, the adoption process, paperwork, and mother's consent had already been under way for months, and this was not the beginning of the process. It was the very last step. All they needed from Antonia today was a signature, or a verbal consent, because the final dossier would state that she couldn't read or write.

"What's happening?" Berenice asked.

"Mi hija," Antonia finally addressed her daughter. "You're going to stay here for the night, but tomorrow I'll come and get you," she lied.

"But I don't want to stay here," the girl probably protested. "I want to go and see the city and visit my aunt."

Antonia turned to Doña Cesy. "I don't want to give her up." Though in a meek voice, the mother launched a last-ditch effort to keep her daughter. "The girl is already older. There must be a mistake."

"No," Cesy answered, fully composed. "Don't worry, la niña va bien." The girl will be fine. She continued to use language that would shield Bereníce from what was actually happening.

"Remember, they'll pay you," Cesy added, rubbing her fingers together and uttering a promise that Antonia had already heard several times from this woman.

"Ay, no. Eeeeeh!" Antonia protested. "Me da lástima." It hurts me. The girl began to cry.

"See, look at her now!" Cassandra jumped in. "We should take her and look after her because she's crying."

And with that Cassandra took Bereníce by the hand and walked her out the door, where a car was waiting. There was no physical resistance, kicking, or screaming. Antonia did not rise up out of her chair and follow the girl. What was done was done. She had voluntarily given up her child.

Cassandra opened a rear door for Bereníce, and the girl, her eyes still moist, climbed inside. This poor, confused Guatemalan girl just shy of eight years old was now officially the property of Hogar Nuevo Día and eligible to be adopted by a family from the United States of America. A turn of the key, the engine started, and the car pulled away.

But what was this? Two blocks away from Cassandra's office, as the car headed south on Antigua's main street, ironically in the direction of the road that leads to Escuintla and Tiquisate, Bereníce saw two boys chasing the car, waving at her.

"¡Mis hermanos!" she realized. My brothers! She crawled to the back of the car and planted her face against the rear window, the tears gushing forth now, for it was the rainy season, and she pronounced their names. "Maynor! William!" The car reached the end of the cobble-stone street and found pavement. It sped up.

Understanding that they would be gone in a matter of seconds, Bereníce raised her right hand and waved good-bye to her brothers.

Maynor and William saw her outstretched palm, and they waved too, as if that would somehow bring back their little sister, but to no avail. The car disappeared from view.

She was gone.

4 ❧ Shopping for Kids

The Northwest Airlines late flight from Detroit headed up over Michigan, the state shaped like an open right hand, and needed only forty minutes to reach Traverse City, a town of about fifteen thousand, located at the crux of where the pinkie finger and the ring finger meet. The plane circled once over Cherry Capitol Airport and then touched down on a runway clear of the crusty white tundra surrounding it for miles. By the time they taxied up to the gate, Judy Barrett, her eleven-year-old twins, Amelia and Elizabeth, and her husband, Bob Walters, had noticed the dismal, dark landscape awaiting them outside and already dreaded disembarking and facing the toughest stretch of the northern Midwest's brutal winter. It was early January 2000, and they wouldn't see green fields for another three or four months. Sure, they were glad to be home, and relieved, but this was the dreariest time of the year in Traverse City, the months they endured to be able to enjoy a radiant summer and fall.

The family had suffered through one heck of a travel day that began before dawn in lush, warm Guatemala, paused for long and cumbersome layovers in Houston and Detroit, and finally ended here in Traverse City. Needless to say, their bodies were certainly happy to be back home. But while their brains just wanted to turn on the television, raid the refrigerator, hit the pillow, and grab hold of what was familiar, their hearts trailed behind somewhere along the itinerary of airports like lost luggage.

The tiny airport with only two check-in gates was quiet this late in the evening, as usual, and once Judy, Bob, Amelia, and Elizabeth descended the escalator to the ground level and retrieved the checked luggage from their week-and-a-half-long trip to Guatemala, it didn't take them more than a minute before they were outside in the bitter January air, next to the station wagon, waiting for Bob to find his keys.

He fished for them in the right front pocket of his jeans, but his hands were already freezing cold. Fatigued and unused to international travel, Bob was on the verge of throwing down his arms in surrender. This was usually when one of the twins would jump in and lodge a complaint about being hungry or bored, or about how inept their parents were at simple tasks. But for some reason Amelia and Elizabeth were stone-cold silent, standing there like frozen zombies in the January air. And it wasn't just the arduous journey that had sapped their energy, for here in the parking lot of Cherry Capitol Airport, with no one else around to witness, a family crisis was unfolding.

There was no fighting over who got to sit in the front seat and no jubilation when Bob turned the heat on full blast and, within seconds, the comforting air reached four faces and eight hands. Bob pulled out of the parking lot and headed north on the airport's two-lane entrance and exit road, crossed the railroad tracks, and paused at the blinking red stoplight at the intersection of US-31, the highway that runs up the west coast of the state toward the Mackinac Bridge. No traffic was coming from either direction this late at night, but somehow he couldn't move forward, his right foot suspended two inches shy of the gas pedal. Bob and his family were stuck in time.

Judy looked out through the windshield and saw nothing but bare trees and snowdrifts piled up on the side of the road. The sky above was gray and dark. It depressed her that only a day ago they had been looking at radiant purple bougainvillea flowers and green vines spilling over a cream-colored wall, below which a short, squat Indian woman was washing clothes in a cistern. She could still hear the sound of children playing and wished she was back in the courtyard of the orphanage, surrounded once again by a dozen kids all looking up at them with those longing, if not pathetic, stares, crying out, "¡A mí! ¡A mí!" Pick me! Pick me!

But the Barrett-Walters family had not been able to "pick" a child the week before in Antigua, Guatemala. Now they had traveled thousands of miles in the past sixteen hours, and that gnawing sense of guilt from their indecision had followed them here to the upper reaches of the United States, in a town not on some maps, like a horrible nightmare. Judy couldn't help but close her eyes and watch that scene rewind and play, over and over again. When she gazed into the rearview mirror above the windshield, did she see two kids in the backseat . . . or more?

A car horn behind them honked, telling Bob that it was time to move along. He turned left onto US-31 and pulled into the right lane, true to character, letting the impatient driver pass him on the left. There was no hurry now, since the Barrett-Walters family was stuck between two worlds. They drove by several boarded-up beach hotels that had left their neon welcome signs on, even though they wouldn't see guests until the suburban Chicago and Detroit tourists arrived in June. The entrance to Northwestern Michigan Community College appeared and disappeared, and the illuminated sign for Arby's roast beef sandwiches on the left side of the street reminded Bob that it was time to tap the right blinker.

Amid a complete and terrible silence (had anyone even spoken since the stewardess offered them drinks on the flight from Detroit?), Bob let his instincts guide them home. The car turned right onto Center Road and drove north on Old Mission Peninsula, past the naked cherry and apple orchards inundated by snow, and crested a rise overlooking the ice covering East Grand Traverse Bay and the open waters of Lake Michigan beyond. Could a Guatemalan child from a temperate climate survive a winter here?

Finally, a right-hand turn onto Timberlane Drive, two miles more, and Bob sighed in relief to see that in their absence their driveway had been plowed. A foot of snow covered the roof of their house, a dozen icicles hung over the garage door, and Bob, a retired forester with the Department of Natural Resources, recognized squirrel tracks in the snow on the porch. Everything looked just as it did when they had left only ten days ago, of course. Were they expecting a difference? Were they expecting an obvious sign in front of their home that they had returned empty-handed? Because, inside each one of them, the world had changed forever.

ैे

Not until she sank into the comfortable leather couch downstairs and faced the television did Judy open her mouth and begin releasing her bottled-up emotions.

"I just thought it would be easy once we got there and saw the little girl's face. I thought we'd fall in love at first sight—you know, like you see in all those TV drama documentaries."

"Yeah, me too," answered Bob, his tall, stoic figure standing over Judy, rubbing her shoulders.

It was an American named Clayton Phelpers who ran an orphanage in Antigua called Hogar Nuevo Día who had replied when Judy began e-mailing Guatemala to inquire about older girls to be adopted. Clayton wrote to Judy that they had a well-behaved, adorable seven-year-old girl (though they weren't entirely sure of her age) available named Eleanor Patricia, and that prompted Judy and Bob to book four plane tickets to Guatemala. They weren't entirely sure they wanted to go through with this, and that's why the twins needed to be there to help make the gut decision.

In their minds, at least, the Barrett-Walters family had been ready to adopt when they left Michigan a few days after Christmas in 1999. But once on the ground, once they had witnessed dozens of kids pleading for a family, once they realized the pain and malnutrition that plague Guatemala's youth, once the moment came to add another member to their happy little gringo clan, they just froze. And Amelia and Elizabeth weren't any help, either. To them, the kids running around the orphanage yard, ducking under clotheslines and booting soccer balls half their size, were third world specimens of poverty, not potential siblings.

"I was expecting this trip to leave no questions in our minds," reflected Bob, now sitting on the couch next to Judy in their living room in Michigan. "But all of a sudden here we were wondering whether we wanted to add another kid to the house. Does she talk too loud? Does she run around too much? This is what you'd notice in other kids, but not your own child. It's clear to me now that at the orphanage we were looking at all the potential problems."

"Yeah, we were hypertuned in to everything it is that kids do," Judy concurred. "Is she too this? Is she too that? In a way, we were shopping."

"It just wasn't as obvious as I thought it would be," said Bob. "I mean, with the twins, they were part of the package. I married you, and adopted them as well. But if we adopt that girl from Guatemala, do we inherit the weight of the country's problems on our shoulders?"

Judy could imagine the little girl's pretty brown face on the dark television screen in front of her even though it was turned off. The girl was wearing a pink shirt and dark blue jeans, and below her beautiful dark eyebrows was the unmistakable look of longing. Judy knew so little about this girl: her name, Eleanor Patricia Bereníce Ortiz (she was called "Patricia" or "Patty" at the orphanage); her age, approximately eight; where she was from, Guatemala's southern coast; her family history—her mother, a "domestic worker," had arrived about six months before along with two rowdy and misbehaving older brothers to drop her off. So little information, yet she was supposed to claim Patricia as her daughter!

The girl's face had lit up when she saw the four gringos walk into the courtyard of the orphanage. She ran over to Papa Clayton, the only father figure she knew, and asked him, "¿Mis padres? ¿Son mis padres?" Are these my parents? How did she know this? Had someone at Hogar Nuevo Día tipped her off that a prospective family was coming to see her? The adoption paperwork was just in the beginning stages. In fact, Judy and Bob hadn't even completed their home study with the social worker yet. Or did Patricia sense the four sets of eyes on her, studying her, for any faults or scars?

She spent a few days with the Barrett-Walters family in their room at the Radisson Hotel, not far from Hogar Nuevo Día, just south of town on the road heading out toward Escuintla on Guatemala's southwestern coast. Patty seemed to get along well with Amelia and Elizabeth as they played and laughed, together in the hotel pool. In spite of the language barrier, she showed no signs of anger or social handicaps. Still, Judy and Bob couldn't help but notice the tiny burn marks on Patty's legs and torso. Had someone been beating her? they wondered.

They took her to Lago de Atitlán, the pride of the Mayan Indian highlands, where an entire volcano had collapsed some three thousand years ago and a magnificent freshwater lake had taken its place. Aldous Huxley called Atitlán the most beautiful lake in the world when he visited there, and certain indigenous villages around its perimeter boasted the toughest resistance to the military during the civil war. Any Guatemalan child would be proud of her heritage, standing in front of its azure waters.

But that made little difference when Judy took Patty back to the orphanage to drop her off, the doubt and shame clearly visible in the potential mother's eyes. The girl cried a river of tears when she was abandoned a second time, for this was her chance at a good home with a loving family in *El Norte* slipping through her fingers. Judy knew what Patty wanted to hear, but she couldn't bring herself to say those magic words: "We'll be back."

Bob would have no part in the good-bye. He waited among the lush plants and foliage at the greenhouse hotel Quinta de las Flores, a setting more in keeping with his comfort level. This trip had already been trying enough for him, as he battled parasites and a headache, and the realization that tomorrow's flight home, with Patty back at the orphanage, was going to be the moral equivalent of a journey through hell.

❧

"Dumb shits!" Karen Grettenberger pronounced into the telephone without even a pause to reflect on the predicament Judy Barrett was describing. "Love *follows* commitment. You have to make the commitment *first*!"

The voice of Karen's husband, Lou, the Methodist minister, back in Traverse City, sounded over the speakerphone. "We understand what you two are going through, but you can't expect Patty to seem like the perfect child, or even *your* child, yet," he consoled Judy. "She's been stuck in a Guatemalan orphanage for the last year. She doesn't understand your language, your customs, or why you are down there. She wants a home. She *deserves* a home."

"When we adopt, we aren't window-shopping. That's the wrong way to go about it. You have to commit to the child first, before you know her, before you know what she looks like, before you know how smart she is or where she will go to college. The love will follow naturally, I guarantee you, once she is a part of your family back here."

Judy nodded. Of course this was true. Of course she needed to commit to Patty before she would love the girl as a mother should. What did she expect, instant chemistry? She hadn't carried Patty in her womb for nine months. She hadn't endured the pain of labor as she had with Amelia and Elizabeth. How could she expect to feel the same bond with Patty the moment she held her the first time?

But by the time Judy said goodnight and ended the long-distance telephone call to the Grettenbergers from Quinta de las Flores in Antigua, she had already taken Patty to Hogar Nuevo Día and said good-bye. She had already told Clayton Phelpers that she wasn't sure whether her family wanted to adopt, and watched him shrug his shoulders as if to say, "Well, it doesn't work for all." When she shook his hand and thanked him for the visit and the tour he added, "If you change your mind, we'll be here. Guatemala isn't going anywhere, and Patricia isn't getting any younger." And as the taxi took her back to Antigua, Judy knew she would be forever haunted by the image of Patty, standing in the sunny courtyard, asking Clayton if those were her parents who had just arrived.

What did these dead ends mean? Judy thought on the long plane ride the following day. Her abandoned mother who secretly longed her whole life to know *her* own roots, her ex-lover who would never know Amelia and Elizabeth, and Patty, waiting in an orphanage in Guatemala for some family to claim her.

It wasn't until they had arrived in Traverse City that night, driven home through the snowy countryside, talked about the dizzying events of the last week and a half, and finally settled into bed that Bob, the glue that had held her together all these years, made the definitive declaration that settled it all: "There is a little girl rotting in an orphanage down there. What the hell are we thinking? She needs a family!"

Luckily, Judy hadn't yet unpacked. Within a week she was headed back to Guatemala to adopt Eleanor Patricia Bereníce Ortiz, who had been crying almost every night since her birth mother had abandoned her six months earlier.

ॐ

Judy and Bob had needed a sign or some conclusive event to help them make the commitment to adopt Eleanor Patricia Bereníce Ortiz when they visited her at the orphanage in Antigua. This middle-aged adult couple even looked to their preteenage daughters for confirmation, and they weren't able to make the final push until they talked to their humanitarian friends the Grettenbergers and, even then, not until they returned to Michigan, guilt ridden and without having committed to the adopted child. It's important to note that many of the Americans I spoke to who adopted from Guatemala also looked for some kind of justification, a sign that the path they chose was the right one. Some were deeply religious, others not, but many needed outside help to push them to make the final decision. April Hayman, the Tennessee mother who adopted McKenna, the girl from the coffee *fincas* in western Guatemala, had dreamed at night of saving a brown-skinned child from an impoverished country. When April learned that the girl was born on the exact same day that her biological daughter, Peyton Rose, almost drowned in a pool accident in Chattanooga, she believed the hand of her God had bound her to not just any child but a certain little girl in that country.

Other couples found the connection they needed in something as simple as a name. There was a boy whose birth mother had named him after a Guatemalan volcano, and because the adopting parents had once seen that volcano, they decided he was meant for them. Or a couple who wanted to add "Emilia" to their daughter's birth-given name, and when they learned that the girl named "Ava" with whom they were matched up had a twin sister also named Emilia who had died at birth, they called it a sign, and believed this was their way of keeping the memory of the sister alive. Yet another adoptive mother was matched with a girl whose middle name at birth was "Rubi," fitting because both she and the girl were born in July and shared the ruby as a birthstone. Best of all, a woman from Ohio looking for a sign that she and her husband were heading down the right path in adopting from Guatemala quelled her worries when the message in her fortune cookie read, "Great things are coming from a faraway land."

It's also important to remember the deep faith and religious inspirations of many Americans who adopt from abroad. Tennesseans April and Kenny Hayman were only recent examples of a long history of Christians who felt a calling from their God to do what they considered to be saving a child from third world poverty. The years following the Second World War saw a rise in foreign adoption within the United States, and then Harry and Bertha Holt, an Evangelical couple from rural Oregon, adopted eight Korean War orphans after a special act of Congress was passed in 1955. The Holts became pioneers of the movement and facilitated the adoption of hundreds of other Korean children who were fathered by American soldiers and then cast out by their own society once the war ended and the troops returned home. According to Ellen Herman, who runs the Adoption History Project at the University of Oregon, the Holts believed they were doing God's work in bringing these poor children to the United States. "They relied on proxy adoptions and overlooked the minimum standards and investigatory practices endorsed by social workers," she writes on the project's informative Web site. "They asked that their applicants be 'saved persons' who could pay the cost of the children's airfare from

Korea. . . . They were happy to accept couples who had been rejected, for a variety of reasons, by conventional adoption agencies."

But not everyone thought the Holts were doing good work. According to Herman, the U.S. Children's Bureau, the Child Welfare League of America, and the International Social Service tried, and failed, to shut down them down. The Holts were viewed as "dangerous amateurs, throwbacks to the bad old days of charity and sentiment." Herman writes, "For the Holts, family-making required faith and altruism, not social work or regulation, and they found nothing wrong with the idea of Americans adopting foreign children, sight unseen. American childhood, they assumed, was unquestionably superior to childhood in developing nations."

The Holts' contribution to foreign adoption reached a climax on December 27, 1958, when their airplane, *The Flying Tiger*, landed in Portland, Oregon, with 107 Korean children on board who would end up in the hands of American families through the Holt Proxy Adoption Program. Arnold Lyslo, who was there that day and witnessed the reactions to the Korean children, wrote in a letter titled "A Few Impressions of Meeting the Harry Holt Plane, the 'Flying Tiger'":

> I could not help but feel that a few of the adoptive couples were disappointed in their child. The expressions on some of their faces were revealing that perhaps this was not the child that they had dreamed of, and they were still bewildered at the appearance of the child and his inability to make immediate response as they wished. . . . I could only think how different this could have been with the participation of good social agencies who could work with these families to evaluate for their own good and the welfare of the child, their capacity to adopt a Korean child.

"By the early 1960s," Ellen Herman writes, "the Holts responded to pressure from the child welfare establishment . . . and repeated a pattern central to the history of modern adoption: the movement from humanitarian to professionalism and from religion to science."

Another form of adoption in the United States, which was conducted largely across ethnoreligious lines, carries a particularly painful legacy. Beginning in colonial times, throughout the nineteenth century, and all the way up until 1978, when it was outlawed, children were forcibly taken away from Native American families, especially following Anglo-American wars against Native nations. An argument can be made that the outright racism and perceived superiority of white Christian settlers over the indigenous peoples whose land they stole persist today, though subtly, when it's assumed that a childhood in the United States is automatically better than a childhood in, say, Guatemala.

Throughout the twentieth century and beyond, waves of international adoption have almost always followed in the wake of wars and social unrest that leave orphans and extreme poverty behind them. Following the U.S. capitulation in Vietnam, American social workers left Saigon in 1975 with babies in their arms, and the fall of the Iron Curtain in 1989 opened up Russia and other Eastern European countries to Americans looking to adopt. Russia and China are, along with Guatemala, two of the three largest sources of foreign adoption today, largely because of rampant poverty; in the case of China, the central government actually promotes it as a way to control the population and discourage families from raising more than one child.

Guatemala as a booming source of foreign adoption has much to do with the fallout from the terrible civil wars that plagued Central America throughout most of the cold war and the ongoing disparity in wealth, educational levels, and land distribution. Add to that a violent machismo culture, the lack of women's rights, and the racism that continue to plague the country. Fittingly, Guatemalan adoption was also born under the auspices of the church. Many children who survived the military massacres in the western highlands or were separated from their parents in the ensuing and confusing escape march to Mexico during the bloody 1980s found refuge with liberal Catholic nuns who risked their lives to save Mayan Indian children, cared for them in the convents, and sometimes passed them on to loving parents safely outside the country.

ह

"Back to my girl, back to my girl," Judy repeated to herself over and over again like a mantra as she retraced her route of the previous week, back through the airports in Traverse City, Detroit, Houston, and Guatemala City. And even though passing through customs at La Aurora International Airport was as simple as showing your American passport, smiling, and saying, "Buenos días," the fifteen-minute wait must have seemed like an eternity for Judy, as did the hour-long shuttle ride into Antigua.

But once the minibus turned off the highway from the capital and onto 3 Calle, one of Antigua's colonial, romantic, yet bone-jarring cobblestone streets that headed west past the Parque Central, Judy could almost see her daughter's beautiful smile, literally just blocks away. Though the bus jostled her left and right as its tires swerved to avoid potholes and tourists wandering blindly in the middle of the street, Judy felt calm and confident, as if the past few years of her life had been leading her to this moment, this sweet reunion. It was, indeed, like those moments after giving birth.

She wouldn't tell Patty, of course, but the girl was costing her approximately twenty-five thousand dollars—a pretty penny to many Americans, and an unfathomable amount to most Guatemalans. Her store, Wild Birds Unlimited, had made a killing on Beanie Baby sales of late, and that had made this adoption possible.

Now was the time for proposals and happy tears. In the courtyard of Hogar Nuevo Día, on the grassy lawn, near the bougainvillea vines with an Indian woman washing clothes in a cistern and happy kids running around in the sunshine, is where Judy Barrett exorcised her demons from the week before when she had returned to Michigan, empty-handed. One of Clayton's workers brought out Patty, whose first expression was one of surprise when she saw this woman who had left her a week ago, now kneeling on one knee with tears welling up in her eyes.

"Yo quiero estar tu mamá," Judy proposed. Her Spanish grammar was off, and the words were likely not very audible between sobs. But Patty definitely understood the most important word, *mamá*—two beautiful syllables she hadn't been able to formulate together since Antonia had dropped her off here without any forewarning many months before.

Patty nodded her head yes and embraced her new mother. The tears gushed forth in a cascade of emotions now, and if Patty whispered anything into Judy's ears in her sweet foreign language of childhood doubt and the pain of past scars, the meaning of the words was lost, though the sound of her squeaky young voice resonated throughout Judy's body.

They were together now, mother and daughter, and it was Patty's turn to forgive Judy for abandoning her a week ago, even though the girl had been unable to forgive Antonia these many months in the orphanage, for now Judy said the word *siempre*, forever. "We'll be together forever. No one will ever leave you again."

The next five nights together were so joyful and void of problems that, years later, neither one would remember exactly how they were spent. In the jumbled blur of memories were haircuts, hours playing in the pool, trips to the market to buy fresh fruit, excellent cuisine in Antigua's restaurants, and early evenings, sitting together in the Parque Central, watching plumes of water shoot out of the fountain, while Patty rested her head on Judy's lap and called her "Mamá."

Unfortunately, in the adoption world, whereas love follows commitment, the journey to the new home must also follow months of waiting for bureaucratic red tape, as is well known by Judy and any adoptive family who visits their child before the home study is complete and the Procuradora General de la Nación has officially approved the Guatemalan child's right to be claimed by foreign parents. On their e-mail lists, adopting parents often refer to PGN as purgatory, and routinely lend each other shoulders for support as the days and weeks mount before the baby can come home.

At the end of the five days of bliss, Judy had to leave again, which was the culmination of Patty's worst fears. But this time, Judy told her daughter, "Yo voy a regresar." I'll be back. And she meant it. The trust was there now, and Patty knew it was just a matter of time before she had a real home, with a real family, in *El Norte*.

Judy shook Clayton's hand and told him, "I'll be a good mom, I promise." And Patty's mood when she returned to the orphanage for a spell was one of joy and anticipation, for her days in an institution would soon come to an end. The other kids at Hogar Nuevo Día surely felt Patty's excitement and probably shared it with her. But the older ones also realized that with every passing day, and each time one of their fellow relinquished mates left the temporary home with a happy American couple, their own chances at a life with a loving family were getting smaller and smaller. Thus, the *despedidos*, or good-bye parties, often held at Guatemalan orphanages or sometimes even at the upscale touristy hotels in the capital were a delicate balance between tears of joy and sadness: Patty's friends crying because they were sad to see her go and she would never return, but also out of a jealousy in the pits of their little stomachs.

Patricia's dream, her inalienable right as a child, would soon be realized. As social workers all over the United States preach, all children have the right to parents who love them and will feed and take care of them and, if possible, provide them with an education. So this was a win-win situation. An American family that wanted to adopt a child was able to do so, and Patty, institutionalized for almost a year by the time she was able to leave, would finally have a home. A child's right to a good home, international adoption advocates say, overrules the controversy about whether Guatemala's kids are bought and sold as commodities.

Two months later, the Barrett-Walters family had passed their social worker's home study, and Judy, the twins, and her friend Nancy, a high-rolling real estate mogul from southern Michigan, returned to Antigua for a "girls week" spring break. The adoption paperwork was still working its way through the system in Guatemala City, so they couldn't take Patty home yet. This was just a visit. Nevertheless, determined to plant a seed that would one day grow into a classy, feminine

American woman in the little girl who once swept the filthy market floors in an impoverished village in the Costa Sur, Nancy gave Patty a bottle of expensive perfume on the day they had to return to the United States.

And at that very moment, the girl would always remember, an airplane flew overhead, headed north. "It won't be long now," Judy told Patty . . . "Hasta que estamos juntos" . . . until we're together.

5 ❧ Forgotten Land

What happens in the void left by the children who depart Guatemala by the thousands? Does the land pine for them? Do the mothers who gave them up think about them daily, or only once in a while? Perhaps when they see an airplane passing overhead, or when the birthday of their relinquished child comes and goes, or when they see *norteamericanos* shopping for Mayan fabrics in one of Guatemala's artisan markets. "Did my *niña* end up with a family like that?" the biological mother asks herself. "Tall and healthy, confident and wealthy, their travel packs bulging with *dinero*." The children themselves lose a family when they are adopted, and some would argue, a culture, a history, and a landscape, too. But that void begins to disappear the moment they are placed in their cribs in a happy home in the United States: lullabies are sung; English is spoken; the Americanization begins. What about Guatemala itself?

Every day in the Parque Central in Antigua, adopting couples interact with the locals, sometimes through words, or sometimes just through glances that cross cultural barriers. In this *parque* Judy Barrett took her daughter Bereníce after returning in haste to propose to her, and the eight year old whom she now called Ellie rested her head in Judy's lap and called her "Mamá." Most adoptive parents change their child's name to something more American, or often a name that's common in both English and Spanish. Judy and Bob went with "Ellie" because the girl's birth certificate identified her as "Eleanor Patricia Bereníce." They had no idea that she had been called Bereníce throughout her first seven years and Patricia during her time at the *hogar*. For whatever reason, the girl in question never protested or corrected those around her. She seemingly moved from one stage of her life to the next with ease.

It was also the same *parque* where a gay single father from Brooklyn named Ryan took his adopted son, whom he nicknamed "Tank," and where he fended off accusatory looks from Mayan women sitting on nearby park benches selling *jocote* fruit and bananas. "¿Adopción?" they asked Ryan, who understood just enough Spanish to know what was going on. "¿Pero dónde está su madre?" But where's his mother? Indigenous women laughed at the idea of *a man* raising a child by himself . . . and for fear of persecution, homosexuals are forced to remain in the closet in Guatemala.

When April Hayman, the mother of four from Tennessee who adopted McKenna from the coffee region, spent several months living in Antigua waiting to take her daughter home, she didn't weather the same abuse and cross-eyed looks that the Brooklynite Ryan experienced. In touristy areas like Antigua or the villages around Lake Atitlán, the otherwise taboo of brown babies in the hands of white parents was accepted because the locals lived on the money spent by foreigners. When she had her other children, Trey, Chase, Casey, and Peyton Rose, with her in the *parque*, April noticed that she was instantly respected as a good mother. It was the families coming to adopt their first child who faced the tough stares and questions from the local women. Or, God forbid, *una homosexual*! Under Guatemalan law, gays or lesbians are not legally allowed to adopt, but many attorneys or American social workers will make exceptions and forge the paperwork, or make it appear that a spouse of the opposite sex is involved too. For some it's about protesting a homophobic law; for others it's about the money.

Adopting mothers like April and Judy also knew better than to take their daughters away from the touristy areas and into the traditional rural villages, where stories abound of foreign women being attacked with machetes for getting too close to the local children. Rumors and legends rule the day in rural Guatemala, where the people's legitimate fear of outsiders and their perceived purpose when they visit the country is rooted not only in the way the Spaniards conquered Guatemala, forcing them at knifepoint to adopt Catholicism, but even more so in the brutal civil war, its massacres of tens of thousands of Mayan Indians, and, quite possibly, misinformation about foreigners intentionally spread in the rural highlands. To this day rumors of babies being adopted for their organs persist.

In March 1994—two and a half years before the Guatemalan civil war ended—an environmental activist from California named June Weinstock was attacked by a lynch mob and nearly killed in a highland indigenous community in the state of Alta Verapaz. The locals believed rumors that she had stolen a local woman's child to sell its organs. "What are we if we do not protect our children?" a Maya-Q'eqchi' man was reported to say, following the lynching.

According to Diane M. Nelson's book, *A Finger in the Wound: Body Politics in Quincentennial Guatemala*:

> In the months before [Weinstock's] trip, the Guatemalan press was full of macabre stories of fattening houses and children's bodies found without organs, the body cavity stuffed full of dollars and a thank-you note in English. Guatemalan public discourse, which runs on rumors in the best of cases, was raging on speculation and hearsay about baby trafficking, child snatching, organ transplants, and the nefarious gringos behind it all. . . . Some newspaper accounts linked the rumors directly to the boom in international adoptions, often shady enterprises in which birth mothers are paid pittances to give up their children and gringos take for granted the availability of the child—of course it's better to be raised in the United States than to sell Chiclets in the streets of Guatemala City [meant ironically].

True to form, the American media ran spectacular stories about Weinstock's near-fatal attack in daily newspapers, in *Time*, and on the show *20/20*—coverage that, Nelson writes, portrayed the indigenous people as savages, thus contributing to the country's vicious cycle of racism. Some opined that the mob attacks and unfounded accusations of organ theft were part of the right-wing Guatemalan military's efforts to scare the indigenous population and "create a climate of instability to human rights monitors" (who were coming from outside Guatemala and posed an innate threat to the military's war effort).

In her book, which describes indigenous and Ladino identity politics in Guatemala in the early '90s, the waning days of the civil war and the five hundredth anniversary of the arrival of the first conquistador, Christopher Columbus, in the Americas, Nelson went on to question whether rumors of organ snatching were really all that inaccurate:

> In a "third-world country" like Guatemala, which suffers from neoliberal policies imposed by the International Monetary Fund, and where infant mortality among the Maya is over fifty per one thousand births, how metaphorical *is* it to claim that a child has died because North Americans stole its organs? . . . Such rumors are often extremely clear readings of neocolonial transnational power relationships.

A decade later, the fear of foreigners had hardly dissipated. When mud slides wrought by Hurricane Stan in the fall of 2005 killed thousands of Guatemalans and left about twenty-five children orphaned in the extremely poor village of Panabaj, just a kilometer away from the touristy hot spot of Santiago on the shores of Lake Atitlán (where the military had carried out a massacre fifteen years earlier), the villagers vehemently opposed those kids being adopted by foreigners. In fact, the white UNICEF aid workers who arrived weeks after the tragedy told me they faced fears among the survivors that they had arrived to take the orphans away. And two months after the landslides when I interviewed widows and orphans in the makeshift refugee camp, just up the hill from Panabaj, I faced the same staunch opposition to the children of Atitlán leaving their homes, their culture. The women I spoke to had no conception of the contrast in the quality of life between the United States, or even Antigua, and the dirt paths and tin shacks of Panabaj. But they did convey, through a translator who spoke both Spanish and the local language of Kak'chikel, their belief that no one had the right to rob them of their children, their future.

❧

Yet for April Hayman, the blatant and horrible poverty all around her was enough incentive to save a child by taking her home. On a walk though Antigua's filthy traditional market she had seen children lying on blankets next to tubs of lard filled with flies and adolescent girls chopping open fruit with machetes bigger than themselves. How can children grow up in an environment as dirty and dangerous as this? she thought.

April's conviction was reinforced one day in the *parque* when she walked over to the corner in front of the Banco Industrial, where a group of ex-pat language-school students were lining up in front of the wooden fruit cart to purchase freshly squeezed orange juice for five quetzales (about sixty-six cents) each. In front of the juice cart stood a Mayan woman in a colorful *traje*, albeit stained from days of body sweat. She leaned into a metal hand pump with all her weight and squeezed halves of oranges into a plastic cup. "Mmm, that looks good," April thought out loud, and jumped in line with the other gringos.

The short, plump woman winced whenever she leaned back and pushed all of her body weight into the lever. But she knew her trade well, and it took only a split second for her to crush the half orange. Most of the juice flowed through a thin colander and into the cup below, but once in a while some of it splashed back into her face and onto her dress. The twentysomethings in line laughed, and, fortunately, so did she. There were many things worse in Guatemala than a little sticky orange juice on your chin.

The smell of fresh fruit put April in a lighthearted mood, and she almost literally inhaled a sense of joy for McKenna's native culture.

The sweet aroma filled her nose and then her heart. Forget the revolting market scene and the diseases everywhere, or the racist way the rich treat the poor here, April told herself. Guatemala could be a wonderful place, full of color and tradition and dignity.

But her daydream was interrupted suddenly by the presence of a tiny boy standing in front of her in ragged and soiled clothing, begging her for money. A bony little hand with an open palm hovered around her waist; he had chewed off most of his fingernails. "Un quetzal, un quetzal, por favor. Daaa me aaaal-go . . ." Please, give me something!

There was nothing quaint or funny about this boy, not like the vendors in the Mayan handicraft market whose pandering in broken English sometimes seemed like a comedy sketch, or the fruit woman nearby with orange juice splattering on her chin. This boy was sadly pathetic. A wet stain showed around his crotch, and he wore no shoes, but the most horrifying thing about him was the gray, empty look in his eyes. April looked into his dilated pupils, and from her days working at a medical clinic before she met Kenny, she could tell that this boy was on some sort of drugs. But how could he afford them, given that he clearly had to beg for everything in his pocket?

Ah, that's right. April remembered her translator, Marisol, talking about the street kids who sniffed plastic bags full of cheap glue to kill the pain of their hunger. For a single quetzal these kids could visit any garage or crafts store and stock up on the one thing in their universe that could make them forget, temporarily at least, how poor and pathetic their lives really were. Until the high wore off, and the killed brain cells gave way to the natural instinct for survival, and the boy rose from his drunken stupor and begged for money again.

But how could any parents let their kids do such things, no matter how poor they were themselves? And who on earth would be so cruel as to sell these kids glue, knowing full well they would use it to kill their brains, and their hope? April shook her head in disgust, noticing several other children, both boys and girls, sitting on the steps near the entrance to the Banco Industrial, behind the fruit cart and the woman pumping orange juice. Among them, a girl in her own traditional *traje* looked so tiny and malnourished that a gentle nudge from the security guard standing over her by the bank's iron doors would have seemingly sent her falling onto the cobblestone street. She looked brittle enough to shatter into pieces. The fruit woman's daughter, April guessed. At least this mother brought her daughter to her place of work and looked after her, though seeing the girl's plight was hardly any easier than looking at the boy high on glue.

Fresh-squeezed orange juice in hand, April thought of Norma, and the heart that woman must have had to be able to give up her own daughter to give McKenna a better life. April also remembered the passage from the Bible about the good King Solomon, who receives a baby claimed by two different mothers and orders his men to kill it, knowing full well that the baby's true mother will offer to relinquish her child to save the baby's life. How does that story go?

> Now two prostitutes came to the king and stood before him. One of them said, "My lord, this woman and I live in the same house. I had a baby while she was there with me. The third day after my child was born, this woman also had a baby. We were alone; there was no one in the house but the two of us.
>
> "During the night this woman's son died because she lay on him. So she got up in the middle of the night and took my son from my side while I your servant was asleep. She put him by her breast and put her dead son by my breast. The next morning, I got up to nurse my son—and he was dead! But when I looked at him closely in the morning light, I saw that it wasn't the son I had borne."
>
> The other woman said, "No! The living one is my son; the dead one is yours."
>
> But the first one insisted, "No! The dead one is yours; the living one is mine." And so they argued before the king.
>
> The king said, "This one says, 'My son is alive and your son is dead,' while that one says, 'No! Your son is dead and mine is alive.'"

Then the king said, "Bring me a sword." So they brought a sword for the king. He then gave an order: "Cut the living child in two and give half to one and half to the other."

The woman whose son was alive was filled with compassion for her son and said to the king, "Please, my lord, give her the living baby! Don't kill him!" (1 Kings 3:16-28)

"This is why Norma gave us her little girl," April thought. "To save her." And she returned to Tennessee with her adopted daughter, McKenna, and an eased conscience.

The issue of saviors is a complicated one, however, and Betty Jean Lifton urges adoptive parents to tread carefully when believing they are rescuing their children from a life of poverty or life in an institution. She cautions them against abusing their role as saviors, especially once the children reach the age when they understand that they are adopted:

> We see in these rescue stories, exaggerated or not, the adoptive parents' pride in pulling the Adoptee back from the shadow of death. They have, in that sense, given life to the child and are responsible for its very existence. They do not understand the burden this places on adopted children to be grateful to their saviors. Having been born through adoption, they must be thankful for this second chance, this second life. The "we saved you" story, on one level, is saying: You owe your life to us. Therefore, you must subsume your personal desires to ours. Since we gave birth to you in the only meaningful sense of the word, you belong to us.

❧

Other adoptive parents were reassured through affirmations from Guatemalans that what they were doing was the right thing for their babies. At the La Vista poolside restaurant at the Marriott Hotel in Guatemala City, which caters especially to families adopting children, Lisa and Steve Hinz-Johnson from southeastern Michigan picked a table near the five-man marimba band playing in the far corner so they could capture the scene with their Camcorder. Always courteous and wary of committing a faux pas in a foreign country, Lisa asked the lead marimba player, an older dark-skinned man with white hair and a distinguished, grandfatherly face, if recording them was okay. He smiled and nodded, as he probably does a dozen times every week.

Resting on Steve's shoulder was their soon-to-be adopted daughter, Ava Emilia, who was absolutely tiny for a two-month-old baby. She was so small and delicate, in fact, that blue veins were visible through portions of her skin. The Johnsons were in love with her, but not everyone felt that way. The first American who had the opportunity to adopt Ava asked his agency in disgust, "What the hell is that?" after he looked at the photo they sent him. And so her file had been passed on to the next family.

Ava probably would have died shortly after her premature birth had her biological mother, Marcelina, not put her up for adoption, at least that's what the dossier said. Marcelina had four other kids for whom she probably had enough problems finding food. Ava's father, Diego, wasn't around. When he found out he had impregnated Marcelina, he became agitated and tried to hack off one of her feet with a dull machete. Then he left.

The marimba band took a break, and Francisco Ruin Iñera Juarez, whom Lisa later compared to Morgan Freeman in the way he carried himself, set down his marshmallow-stick *vaquetas* on the xylophone and sauntered over to the family, who had been paying more atten-tion to the traditional Mayan highland music than anyone else in the restaurant. His colleague at the viola, or *contrabajo*, behind the xylophone stood up slowly and acknowledged Steve's clapping with a "Para servirle" (To serve you) before lighting a cigarette.

I could tell that Francisco loved the marimba when I sought out the musician during my time at the Marriott. He told me that he joined the military at an early age to learn the instrument along with the trumpet. The highlight of his career was playing at the World's Fair in Queens, New York, right in front of the big globe at the U.S.

Open, in 1964. And he was happy to meet the Johnsons. Many are the tourists who record him on video, but few are those who sit close enough to engage in conversation.

Lisa made it known that she spoke Spanish, but Francisco had already laid eyes on Ava, whose name means "bird" in Greek, and at this moment she was as delicate as one. He asked how old she was. Two months.

"She had a twin sister who died at birth," Lisa added.

The old man's eyes grew moist.

"She weighed only two pounds when she was born, but now she seems to be eating and doing well."

Francisco just stared. Then he inched a little closer, slowly, like he was about to touch a wounded bird, and placed his hand on her head, on her mass of dark hair. Ava opened her tiny eyes and gazed up at him. "Dios va a cuidar a esa niñeta," he blessed her in a soft voice. God will look after this little girl.

❦

Later that week Lisa was pacing the room in a frenzy, breathing so heavily that the windows threatened to fog up. Ava was very sick, and at her age, at her weight, this was nothing to be taken lightly. She seemed to have a mouth infection, and probably a fever, from the local water. Steve had conscientiously sterilized any water they used in her formula, but something must have slipped through the cracks. The hotel doctor knocked on the door.

A fever wasn't too abnormal, he said. She's just very sensitive.

But then Lisa thought to ask him about the funny purple spots on Ava's back. The Johnsons had been nervous wrecks ever since they noticed what they perceived to be bruises. How could they be? they thought. Her foster mother, Carmen, seemed so loving and careful when we met her in the lobby. They even gave *abuela* a few minutes alone with Ava, to say good-bye.

Lisa pulled out a dictionary and looked up the Spanish word for "bruises" to emphasize her point.

"Oh, no," the doctor said in perfect English. "They're just spots. They'll go away eventually." The Johnsons learned later that "Mongolian Spots" are common among Asian, African American, and Latino infants.

"That happens with the *indios* . . . ," he added, using the most condescending term toward Mayan Indians. Lisa rolled her eyes in disgust and prayed that he'd leave the room soon. She had already read about Guatemalan history, past and present, and knew the deep fault lines racism has caused here.

A day later, Ava still had a high fever, so in a last-ditch effort Lisa and Steve asked the housekeeper for help. All they knew about her at that point was that she kept their room impeccably clean, with baby clothes warm and folded, and wet laundry hanging over chairs. But they hadn't even met her yet.

Lisa knew that many of the Guatemalan women who give their babies up for adoption are housekeepers, or at least that's what the attorneys write in the dossier if the biological mothers have more embarrassing jobs, like offering sex for money. She figured that at least this woman knew how to take care of one of her own.

In walked the *camarera*, the maid, who actually apologized, "I'm sorry she's so sick." She unfolded a blanket and wrapped Ava in a tight swaddle—so tight it made Lisa cringe. Then she held the baby and rocked her back and forth. "Shh, shh," the housekeeper said. "Te quiero, te quiero, te quiero," she performed a rhythmic mantra. I love you, I love you, I love you.

Literally, within twenty seconds, Ava was fast asleep.

Lisa thanked the *camarera* a million times and promised to repeat exactly what she had done. The housekeeper said she had her own child at home. Of course.

The next day when the Johnsons returned to the room to pack up their things and go home, they found that the housekeeper had left two notes: one on the table thanking them for their large tips all week, and the other at the bottom of Ava's crib:

Sabes, bebé. Dios te ha bendecido con tus papás. Sabes, ellos te áman. Y yo, también. —Camarera. (You know, baby. God has blessed you with your parents. You know, they love you. And I do too. —Housekeeper)

She didn't even feel worthy enough to sign her name, Lisa thought. She was an angel. "It just broke my heart."

6 &# An American Girl

Following fourteen-year-old Ellie Walters into her bedroom was like getting a private tour through an art gallery. She pointed out each poster and medal on the wall with pride and blushed in embarrassment when I noticed and began reading the notes her friends had written to her.

There was a picture on the soft white wall of the pop diva Beyoncé Knowles when she was still a member of Destiny's Child. Next to it Jennifer Lopez parted her lips in a seductive smile. On the other side of the doorway, Michael Jordan stuck out his tongue as he skied for another dunk. In pencil Ellie had drawn an impressive portrait of Alicia Keys, not forgetting the stylish cap and her telltale big loopy earrings. "I just like these famous people," she told me.

Ellie's fourth session at the Interlochen Arts Academy summer camp had just ended, and I could tell she'd had a great time that year. Photo after photo of Ellie and her camp friends were taped on the wall above her bed. In one she was twisting her fingers together, forming a pretend gang sign. In another she had her arm around Kaziah, a cabin roommate from Washington DC. There was also a photo of Ellie standing in front of a hotel in Guatemala just before she was adopted, and another of her at Disney World, smiling into the camera—the prototypical American kid, I thought.

When she lay on her left side, on the blanket with a tiger drawn on it, and stared at the opposite wall, Ellie saw medals from playing basketball and volleyball at her local middle school. Behind her was the collage her friend Laura had made for her. It was a series of images cut out of magazines and glued to a poster board: the Star Spangled Banner with "Proud to be an American" written on it; a cross with "God bless you, babe"; two mermaids, one blonde and one brunette, dancing in hoops; and a letter . . . "Dear Ellie, I'm so glad you came to us (us or U.S.? I wondered). I don't know what I'd do without you, girl. I love you and you are so kool. You have a great voice and are very pretty. I mean it. Thanks for being my friend and I hope we'll always be friends and maybe we'll be singers together. Yippee! I love you." Next to the collage were a T-shirt and a duffel bag, both signed by her camp friends at Interlochen. The words *Safe Sex* were written on the bag.

My eyes settled on a beauty display and makeup kit in one corner of the room next to a stack of *Teen People* and *Glamour* magazines. "I'm not very girly," Ellie assured me, "at least not when I'm playing basketball."

But what caught my eye about Ellie's room is that most of the pictures on her walls were of famous black people. I pointed that out to Ellie, making her blush. "Are you more attracted to African Americans?"

Northern Michigan, the region where Ellie was growing up and where my family also lived, was extremely homogenous and white. Mostly German, Polish, Irish, and English farming immigrants settled this rural part of the Midwest, and to see people of color you had to drive downstate to cities like Grand Rapids, Flint, or Detroit. Or you had to turn on the television. So anybody of a different skin color certainly stuck out here.

The second time Ellie, Judy, and I met, at a country restaurant near Interlochen called the Hofbrau, I remembered her telling me that people often called her black. "They can't tell if I'm Mexican, Hawaiian, or whatever," she said, though not in a tone of voice that suggested she was hurt by her minority status. She couldn't think of any times she had been ostracized because of her skin color, and I got the feeling Ellie was actually proud of being different.

"She's a little gringa now, an American," Judy summarized when

Ellie went to the bathroom. "She's very popular among other kids because in our culture it helps to be beautiful and physically a good athlete and a good artist. She's well put-together, my girl. Breathtaking, really."

"I hope you guys don't mind me saying this," Ellie said when she returned to our table. "I don't really like white people all that much. I'm tired of them being everywhere." Judy and I tried to avoid laughing. "On TV I see black people in high schools, but in *my* school there are only white kids.

"I'm obsessed with black people. When I first moved into the cabin at camp the other girls thought I was black, and that was so cool. When I hang out with people, like Kaziah, I feel like I'm part of them. They're really talented. They can break-dance or rap or play basketball, like those people on MTV. I want to be famous like them someday."

❧

I heard some of the same sentiments expressed when I visited Kari, a thirty-two-year-old woman who was adopted from Guatemala at seven years old, like Ellie, and now lived in Detroit with her husband, Brent, an African American. Kari's mother, Nancy, was a social worker who had worked with international adoption for decades, and when she heard that Kari had been abandoned on a street corner in Guatemala near an orphanage with no trace of any family members, she couldn't resist. Nancy bought her a big white stuffed doll and brought Kari back to Michigan.

Mother and daughter visited Guatemala City again as a high school graduation present. They located the street corner where Kari had been abandoned, and they stayed at the same room at the Casa Grande hotel, near the American Embassy, where Nancy had first tucked Kari into bed at night. On that trip Kari remembered things from the past, like a coloring book and corn tamales. She remembered taking the beef patty out of a hamburger in favor of eating just the bun (she would later become a vegetarian), and she dreamed she had an older brother.

But the nineteen-year-old felt terribly guilty each time a Guatemalan approached her and spoke Spanish. She didn't understand a thing, and she felt as if she had let her country down. "I acted and dressed like an American, but everyone told me that I should speak the language."

Kari had become an American, of course. She grew up in suburbia, attended college after the visit to Guatemala, and met her first boyfriend, an African American, at a basketball game. People didn't treat her differently and only asked where she was *from* if they saw her with her Caucasian mother or Nancy's other adopted children, from Vietnam and India. Yet she told me that even before Brent, she had only dated and been attracted to black men, though she couldn't explain why. "There's a connection. I don't know what it is, but I can feel it."

When Kari and Brent got married, their wedding was outdoors, at Nancy's cottage overlooking Lake Huron, in southeastern Michigan. The ceremony was a mix of different cultural traditions. As they said the vows, Kari and Brent held a long Guatemalan silver necklace and wrapped it around their hands to join them for life. And once they had been pronounced husband and wife, the happy interracial couple jumped over a broom on the ground in front of them to honor an African tradition that, according to Nancy, symbolized sweeping out the remnants of their old lives and jumping from singleness into a life together. The broom was decorated with colorful flowers, probably from Guatemala, and afterward they all sang a Spanish lullaby.

❧

It is a strange dance these children perform as they move from one culture to the next, one identity to the next. No need to beg on the dirty streets for food any longer, for now they have the right to beg their parents for expensive Christmas presents. Judy Barrett remembers when she called for Ellie up in her bedroom, the polite Guatemalan girl used to reply, "¿Que manda?" What is your command? But now the response is an annoyed "*What?*" which Ellie probably learned from her sisters.

Suddenly they find themselves like Kari, married and living in a suburban duplex with two kids who play video games after school and beg their parents to order Chinese food from down the street.

It seems every corner of America has one now: a child adopted from Guatemala. If it's a tiny village where the population is predominantly white, the tyke may attract stares and awkward questions while sitting in the child's seat of a shopping cart in the local supermarket. "Is that your baby?" or "Where did you find that little thing?" Or if it's an urban area, there may be a group of a half-dozen families who meet once a week at someone's home or at the food court of the local mall so their little adoptees can play together and so the mothers can swap stories of their trips to Central America. "We were lost in the market in Antigua, and the smells . . ." or "The maid at the Marriott in the capitol was so helpful. She knew just what so-and-so needed . . ."

Nancy and Jeff Bykerk, who have adopted six kids, four from Guatemala, in addition to their four biological children, live in a big house out in the vast expanses of cornfields and freshly mowed gigantic lawns south of Grand Rapids, and that's where they throw the Fiesta Guatemala every summer. The picnic gathering has become a wildly popular event among Michigan families who have adopted from Guatemala, and the same crowd returns year after year to watch each other's kids grow.

The Bykerks order catered Mexican food and place the tacos and ground beef and cheese and vegetables buffet style out on tables in front of their two-car garage. Their guests, some years more than a hundred in number, sit on the lawn or beside the pool with paper plates in their laps, trying to keep track of their toddlers running all over the property while at the same time avoiding the danger of spilling taco juice on their chins and summer shirts.

After dinner, Jeff hangs a piñata shaped like an electric guitar from the basketball hoop near the garage, and the dozens of children, some Guatemalan, some Chinese, some white American, some halfway in between, line up to take a whack at it with a stick Jeff gives them. It takes a good while, but when the piñata finally breaks, the kids dash under the basket and fall on their hands and knees to retrieve the Jolly Ranchers, Hershey's Kisses, Reese's Peanut Butter Cups, and all kinds of other American junk food that fall from above.

But when I attended the Fiesta Guatemala in June 2005, the image that struck me the most and captured the whole beautiful hilarity of these adopted kids wandering between two worlds was when I watched four brown-skinned boys who looked as if they were between three and five years old jumping around together on a trampoline in blue-and-white Guatemalan national soccer team jerseys. Their happy Caucasian parents formed a semicircle around them, clapping and cheering them on and taking pictures with digital cameras. The boys' facial features were partly Mayan Indian and partly Hispanic—*Ladino* is the Guatemalan term—and they shouted back to their parents in toddler English with slight accents. Directly behind them was an empty baseball field, the groomed dirt infield forming a perfect diamond, and beyond that, miles and miles of cornfields.

₹

Every adopting family does whatever is in its power to make the new child feel welcome and, if they are older, help the child integrate into and jell with the new environment. When it came to Ellie, Judy Barrett and Bob Walters were no exception. Judy asked her twin daughters, Amelia and Elizabeth, to pick out a Samantha Doll at a local store for their soon-to-be sister, and they sent it to the girl who still went by the name Patricia at Hogar Nuevo Día in Antigua, while they waited for the adoption paperwork to be completed. Finally, on that day in July 2000 when Ellie returned to Michigan with Judy, the girl was so excited that she didn't sleep a wink on any of the three flights: Guatemala City to Dallas, Dallas to Detroit, or Detroit to Traverse City. She just smiled and held on tight to her Samantha Doll, the first gift from her new sisters.

Of course, times were not always easy for the girl. Once the initial excitement of a new place and a new home wore off and Ellie felt comfortable enough with Judy to share her feelings, the truth behind her late-night crying and pounding the pillow began to emerge. "Why did my mother abandon me?" she pleaded. And Judy would hug her and notice the burn marks on her arms and legs, and slowly pry open the truth about Ellie's biological mother, Antonia, just enough to get a glimpse of the darkness in the girl's past and shed a little light on that dark lonely cellar.

A prostitute . . . she watched her mom have sex with other men . . . the father who abandoned them . . . the witchcraft in a vain attempt to bring him back . . . the lies and the abandonment . . . both happy times and sad times at the *hogar*. Many of the stories emerged through Ellie's therapeutic notepad sketches. She was a talented drawer, Judy noticed right away, but why did all her characters have erect penises and nipples?

Judy waited for news, or a sign, that Ellie had been sexually abused. And then one day, after hours of acute silence from the now nine-year-old girl, Ellie broke down and said, "Mom, I'm sorry, but I'm gay."

Judy could hardly control her laughter. "What do you mean you're gay? Ellie, you're way too young to think about stuff like that."

"But the people at the orphanage said that I'm gay, and they said that's bad."

"Well, when you are older do you want a man or a woman to date or marry?"

"Uh, a man, I guess."

The story emerges that Ellie and another young girl used to lie in bed together, facing each other, at Hogar Nuevo Día, and play kissy-face, or at least as much as eight year olds know how to do. But the maid caught them and told the girls they were sinners: they were gay, and if they didn't stop that they would never find a family.

"Ridiculous," Judy told Ellie. "You are not in that orphanage anymore, and you'll never have to go back there. You're part of our family now, and this is your home." And slowly, the evenings when Judy would hear Ellie pounding the pillow in weeping fits were fewer and further apart, until she asked about her biological family only every six months or so.

In the early days especially, Ellie needed someone around who spoke and understood rudimentary Spanish, and Judy could just get by with what she had learned when she lived in Ecuador in her twenties. That language bond was like the breast milk they would have shared had Judy actually birthed Ellie, the mother liked to say.

Oh, but Ellie loved that Samantha Doll. A little more than a year after she came home to Traverse City Ellie was taken to a shopping mall to have her American Girl picture taken with Samantha in her arms. A mock promotional advertisement using the American Girl photo was framed and mounted on the piano, just outside of Ellie's bedroom. The text reads: "Samantha's Ice Cream Social. American Girl event, September 9 and 10, 2001. Cover story: 'Ellie Walters attends Samantha's party.' Exclusive: 'Girls share stories about their dolls.'" What better way to integrate someone into our culture than to have her pose for a photo as the typical American teenager?

So on September 10, 2001, Ellie fictionally attended Samantha's ice cream social, her metaphorical rite of passage to become an American girl. It was the next morning, of course, when every American would remember where they were when the planes hit the Twin Towers, and for many that title "American" would take on a whole new meaning.

Sometime after that, Ellie was asked to write an essay for school about identity. Judy cringed when she thought of what that self-exploration would do to her daughter, but her fears turned to joy when Ellie centered her piece around the statement: "And now I'm a Maya *and* a Gringa." On occasion, though, Judy would still hear Ellie awake at night weeping, asking herself that same question, "Why?" And she vowed to help her daughter find the answer.

Lifton captured the pain of abandonment that Ellie still felt:

The Adoptee is a genetic stranger accepted into a biologically unrelated family *as if* he or she were part of it; in other words, the Adoptee is a product of social engineering. . . . Those well-meaning "experts" who set up the institution of adoption as a convenience to serve children who needed families and families who needed children, never questioned the psychological validity of the veil that would cover the past like a shroud. In a nation of immigrants it was assumed that anyone could begin again under any conditions; that, if necessary, one could dispense with one's genetic and historical roots as easily as man had dispensed with his tail. It was an Age of Optimism, preceding Auden's Age of Anxiety, and Haley's Age of Roots.

Even if those roots spanned almost the first eight years of one's life.

"Someday we need to find Ellie's birth mother, if she's still alive," Judy would tell Bob, who'd shake his head, wary of that potentially explosive adventure.

1. A Guatemalan adoptee takes a swing at the piñata during the Bykerk
    family's annual "Fiesta" picnic in mid-Michigan, summer 2005.

2. McKenna Hayman, relinquished by her birth mother, Norma, from
Guatemala's western coffee-growing region, with her adoptive mother,
April, at a softball game in Chattanooga, Tennessee, summer 2005.

3. Fourteen-year-old Ellie Walters cuddles with her dog
at home in Traverse City, Michigan, summer 2005.

4. Ellie Walters, just after playing basketball in the front yard, poses with her adoptive mother, Judy Barrett, at their home in Traverse City, Michigan, summer 2005.

5. *(top)* Judy Barrett shares tears, and smiles, with Antonia Cubillas and her son Maynor at the Hotel Familiar in Tiquisate, Guatemala, fall 2005, just after they learned what had become of the girl who was given up seven years earlier.

6. *(bottom)* Adoptive mother Judy shows pictures of Ellie to a happy and curious birth mother, Antonia, during their first meeting at the Hotel Familiar.

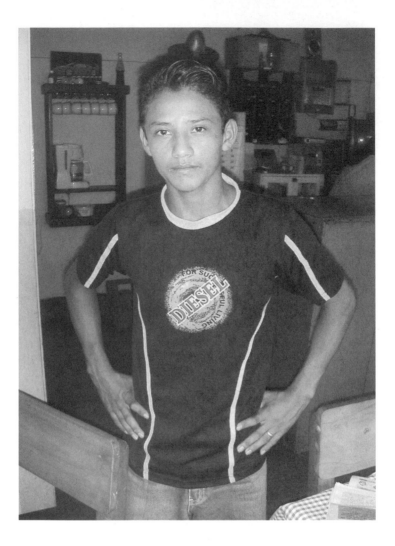

7. Maynor Ortiz Gonzalez, Ellie's oldest brother, was overcome with emotion to learn about his sister ("Bereníce"), and he already pined to see her again.

8. The children Maynor, William, Bereníce, and Erik sharing a birthday cake in the happier days before the family was split apart, date unknown.

9. Antonia Cubillas in her rustic home outside of Tiquisate, shortly after meeting Judy for the first time, fall 2005.

10. William, Maynor, and Antonia's partner, Wagner, outside of their home, waiting for Hurricane Stan's torrential downpour to stop, fall 2005.

11. The effects of Hurricane Stan on Guatemala's
Highway 1 in the western highlands.

12. Gerónimo Mendez ("Chomo"), the public record keeper in Tiquisate, Guatemala, who proved instrumental in finding Antonia, fall 2005.

13. Interviewing survivors and orphans of the mud slide that destroyed Panabáj, Atitlán, during Hurricane Stan.

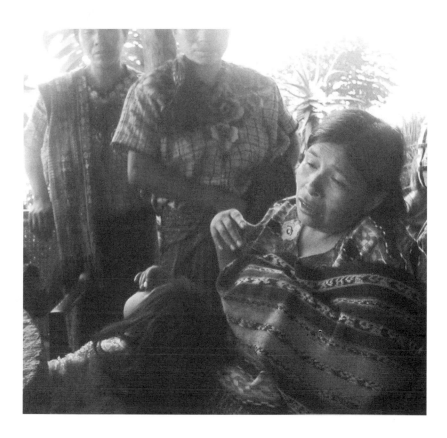

14. Grieving survivors of the mud slide that destroyed Panabáj.

15. A makeshift memorial built where the village of Panabáj once stood, at the foot of the volcano that unleashed the mud slide.

16. Ellie Walters relaxes in a hammock at a resort on Guatemala's Pacific coast, the day before her reunion with her birth family, February 2006.

17. William and a well-dressed Maynor walking through the cobblestone streets of Antigua en route to the reunion with their little sister, Ellie.

18. Antonia, her eldest daughter, Maritza, and her partner, Wagner, en route to the reunion with Ellie.

19. Antonia, in the courtyard of the hotel La Capilla, the moment she
sees Ellie, whom she gave up for adoption seven years earlier.

20. Ellie embraces Antonia in the courtyard of the hotel.

21. Ellie smiles as she sees her two mothers, Judy and Antonia, together for the first time.

22. Maynor cries hard as he embraces the little sister he lost seven years earlier.

23. Just before seviche is served at La Capilla,
    Antonia stares with pride at Ellie.

24. Ellie's entire family relaxes on a bed at La Capilla
following the emotional reunion.

25. Ellie and William show off their moves to Reggaeton
music in Antigua the night of their reunion.

26. Ellie and Maynor share a slow dance at a club
   in Antigua the night of their reunion.

27. Reunited siblings Maynor and Ellie share a moment in the Parque Central in Antigua. Later that day, their mother, Antonia, would return to Tiquisate by bus, and the kids would hatch a plan to escape and avoid being separated again.

PART 2 ❧ *The Return*

7 ❧ Searching for Antonia

The quest to find Ellie's birth mother officially begins on the evening of August 23, 2005, when Judy Barrett and Bob Walters invite me to dinner at their house outside of Traverse City. I have already met and interviewed Judy and Ellie twice this summer, both times at the Interlochen Arts Academy where Ellie attended music camp, and by late August Judy trusts me enough to pass along all the information she has on the woman we know as "Antonia," given that I will return to Guatemala in three weeks.

Judy's plan is to fly down and meet me for a week sometime in the fall—if I'm able to locate Antonia's whereabouts, that is.

"Our trip is on the q.t. from Ellie, though, because my desire is to find out if the mother has any interest in future contact," Judy proclaims from the kitchen as she mixes piña coladas for Bob and me, who are sitting at the bar chatting about the logistics of this trip and all the possible outcomes. "Ellie shouldn't know yet, because if things don't go well I don't want her to have her heart broken."

"We don't know what she has told her other kids," Bob adds, playing the role of the more cautious one in the family, just as he did initially, before they adopted Ellie five years ago. This is the first time I have met Bob, so I carefully explain to him my goal of documenting a reunion between an adopted Guatemalan child and the biological mother for my book. I want to gain his trust, too, so I tell him about my time spent in Guatemala and how I understand some of the risks we may face.

"She needs to be respected," Judy adds, referring to Antonia. I note that Judy and Bob have yet to refer to Ellie's biological mother by her first name. The girl has told us she remembers her mother being called "Antonia," but on this night in this household, the name has yet to be spoken. To us, she is still just a phantom figure, lurking somewhere in Central America . . . still alive, and waiting to be found, we hope.

"Ellie doesn't have to know about the whole big world at her tender age." She's just shy of turning fourteen. "If the outcome is that she doesn't want contact, then we raise our girl by keeping the doors open culturally. We can protect her along the way by telling her that things change. In poverty people don't live that long, and that's one of the reasons she was put up for adoption," Judy adds.

One by one, Judy sticks our beverages under the blender, and to avoid competing with its electric hum, we take a break from talking.

"We've got to think about the different scenarios, too." Judy hands Bob and me our drinks and says out loud what we all fear: "Sometimes you find the birth mother and she just wants money."

The downstairs door bangs open, and Ellie and a friend run in from shooting hoops, still recounting the pretty bank shot Ellie nailed. Our conversation stops abruptly, and the three of us sit there looking a little guilty. This evening Ellie is wearing a red Old Navy sweatshirt and green gym shorts with white stripes running up the sides. Like a million kids across the United States, she is bummed that summer vacation will soon come to a close, but she is psyched about the beginning of girls' basketball season.

Ellie knows I am writing a book about Guatemalan adoption, since I have asked her countless questions this summer about what she remembers from her first seven years. Her story is particularly interesting to me because she was that old when she was given up, and because she does remember so much about her former life. That sets her apart from dozens of other Guatemalan adoptees I have met, who are either too young to be interviewed or not particularly interested in sharing their stories with me.

There is even another family in Traverse City with two daughters adopted from Guatemala who are now teenagers. The older one, Cony, is part Mayan Indian and just shy of graduating from high school. She has actually expressed interest in meeting her birth mother again, which can't be said for her younger sister Sarah, who is of Hispanic descent and was abandoned on the streets of Guatemala City, eliminating any hope of finding her family. But though Cony hopes for a reunion, she was relinquished when she was only a few weeks old and has no recollection of her past life. Unlike Ellie, she has no stories to share, and when I asked her one day if she had any memories of Guatemala or if she felt like a minority, her answer was a curt no. She was on her way out the door because her boyfriend, who is white, was picking her up on his motorcycle to take her to the movies.

Ellie's memories, on the other hand, are numerous. She claims that her father abandoned her, Antonia, and three brothers—whose names she pronounces Maynor, William, and Erik—for another woman and forced them to move to a different house. Ellie remembers growing up near a teeming market where buses would come and go, and that sometimes she herself worked in the market. She and her brothers would play in mudflats not far from their house, which meant that there was a river nearby. She remembers Maynor and William being big and strong, while Erik was small and weak. She thinks he might have died.

Judy has already confided in me that Ellie has told her she remembers her mother working as a prostitute, and that sometimes the kids had to watch their mother turning tricks inside the house. Judy has also seen Ellie's sketches—though she is talented for her age—of people, often naked, with erect and voluptuous sexual organs. She is worried that her daughter was sexually abused, even though Ellie has never mentioned it.

As for the abandonment, Ellie remembers an arduously long bus journey, and a friendly woman with money accompanying them, feeding her stories of the exciting places they would visit, as well as an aunt whom Ellie didn't know. "Guatemala!" was the destination, she remembers. Of course, Antonia never told her the real reason for the trip, and Ellie never got a chance to say good-bye, though she does remember waving to her brothers from the backseat of a car as they chased after her, "trying to save me," as Ellie puts it.

But there are glaring problems with Ellie's memories. She claims she is Salvadoran and that her home village is called "Quitisate," near the Guatemalan border. So how was she abandoned, and then adopted, in Guatemala? Long looks at an online map of El Salvador reveal no town by the name of Quitisate, and nothing even close to that name near that country's northern border to Guatemala. Are Ellie's memories as a seven year old false? Or did her birth mother take her north to Guatemala to give her up, and then return to El Salvador (Salvadoran adoptions are very rare, and maybe Antonia knew that)? And how the heck are we going to find Antonia if we aren't even sure what country she's in?

Putting that crucial question aside, we sit down to a tasty dinner of salad, shrimp, rice, steamed vegetables, eggplant, and fresh Lake Michigan salmon that Bob has grilled out on the porch, beyond the sliding glass door.

"What else do you remember about Quitisate?" I ask Ellie, who is sitting next to me.

"There was a big fancy hotel that burned down one time," she says. "Someone threw fireworks into it."

"Did you ever see any tourists? People like us?" Judy jumps in, even more eager than I to solve this riddle.

"Yeah, one time two big, pale white people came walking by. One was holding a camera in their bag. I came running to my mom, asking, 'Who are these people?' She said, 'Just gringos.'"

That doesn't help much, I think. This town clearly isn't a touristy destination, but a couple of gringos have wandered into almost every village on the globe to take pictures at least once. I make note of the fire Ellie remembers. That could be a valuable clue.

Later, after dinner, Judy, Ellie, and I relocate to the plush leather couches downstairs—the same ones where Judy and Bob agonized in January 2000 over whether to adopt. Judy inserts a home video into the vcr that was recorded at Hogar Nuevo Día by some other American couple there to meet their child. The thirteen-year-old Ellie accidentally spills ice cream all over her lap as we watch the poor-quality video of eight-year-old Ellie standing in the courtyard of the Antigua *hogar*, wearing blue jeans and red suspenders with white stars on them while chewing on a candy cane. How patriotically American!

Ellie disappears, and the camera zooms in on a boy named Javier, whose hair is combed forward in a slick. He would later be adopted by a single gay man from Colorado, Judy tells me. "Say '*Hola*,' Javier," a voice cracks. A generic scene follows of potential parents passing out candy to dumbfounded kids. "Santos, can you wave?" a woman's voice says in a deep southern drawl. Crying, a mother holds her new adopted baby for the first time. The camera returns to Ellie, still standing there in the courtyard. "Just wait for Judy," a woman promises. "She'll be here soon."

Onto the screen walks Clayton Phelpers, with sunglasses tied around his neck, wearing white khakis, brown hiking boots, and a plaid shirt. The director of Hogar Nuevo Día looks vibrant and upbeat, giving high fives to all the kids who run up to him saying "Choc-oh-lay" over and over again. Then the screen fades to gray, and we wait five minutes hoping the picture will reappear before switching off the television.

"Well, I guess that's all we have of Hogar Nuevo Día," Judy tells me, disappointed. In the dark room I can hardly see her face, and I wonder if we'll ever find this mysterious woman, Antonia, or if it's even worth searching for her, given the obstacles before us.

Judy switches on a lamp next to the leather couches. She is holding two large manila envelopes in her hand, each one stuffed solid.

"What's in those?" I ask.

"The dossier."

Of course, I think. The official paperwork Judy received from Hogar Nuevo Día and from the pgn, the Guatemalan equivalent of the attorney general's office that approves each adoption. I have seen a half-dozen of these this summer, each one pertaining to a family I have interviewed that has a child from Guatemala. But most of their adoptions have taken place within the past year or two. Ellie left Guatemala in 2000, before the tidal wave of Americans adopting Guatemalan babies began and before that country's government teamed up with the American Embassy to enact new measures ensuring that each adoption was legitimate and that each birth mother was real. I was worried that Judy and Bob hadn't received the information on Ellie, which would include a copy of her birth certificate, her mother's national identification card, and a report filed by a Guatemalan social worker or lawyer on why Antonia was giving her up—all valuable clues that would help us find Ellie's birth mother.

Judy and I spend a half hour poring over the documents, which are mostly in Spanish but with a few corresponding translations in English. And like many of the adoptive families I have interviewed, I find that Judy hasn't read through the details of Ellie's former life. Or if she has, she hasn't committed the facts to memory. This may seem surprising, but in the final stage of an adoption the parents are more likely to pay attention to their new child and file away the paperwork to be read later. Plus, the dossier usually recounts a tale of woe so foreign to middle-class or wealthy American adoptive parents that it's likely many of them are unable to grasp the story on paper in front of them and confuse or overdramatize the facts when they recount them to family members or friends.

Birth mother's full name: "Juana Antonia Cubillas Rodrigues." Height: 1.47 meters, or 4 feet, 10 inches. She weighs 50 kilograms, or 110 pounds (or did at the time of the relinquishment). Her skin is "*morena,*" or brown, her eyes have a "café" color. Her passport is from El Salvador . . . hmm, interesting. But the stamp listing her hometown within El Salvador is illegible . . . "Alcaldia Municipalidad ???????" Darn. Birth mother can't read or write, the document states. The space where she was to sign her own name is simply crossed out.

The dossier moves on to Ellie, who is referred to throughout as Patricia Bereníce. She was given the Guatemalan passport number 138373182 even though she claims to be Salvadoran. That's strange.

Date of birth: October 3, 1991. Place of birth, registered as "Antigua." What? The alarm sounds in my head. That's impossible. She might be from El Salvador or she might be from Guatemala, but she's definitely not from Antigua, the town so full of tourists that its other official language is English.

I smell a rat, and I tell Judy. We know that Ellie spent nearly a year living at the *hogar* in Antigua before she was adopted. During that time someone, somewhere, must have erroneously reported that she was born in Antigua. Why? A human error? Doubtful. Or was this done to elude the bureaucracy? Somewhere along the line Clayton's job would have been easier if Ellie had been officially born there, in the same town as Hogar Nuevo Día and not somewhere else.

Worst of all, if her place of birth is bogus, then what else is forged? Overcome by curiosity, I read on.

Birth certificate: "The undersigned registrar of the Village of Pueblo Nuevo Tiquisate Escuintla Department certifies that Patricia . . ." Tiquisate! That sounds an awful lot like Quitisate, doesn't it? Is it possible that a seven-year-old girl's ears simply got one syllable wrong? I ask Judy.

I continue: "Daughter of Esvin Arnoldo Ortiz Gonzalez and of Juana Antonia Cubillas Rodrigues, born at Tiquisate Hospital, October 3, 1991 at 9:15 a.m." Esvin Arnoldo . . . so that's the name of the father who abandoned his wife and children for another woman. The thought crosses my mind that I might have to find him too to piece the entire story together.

Lawyer: "Cassandra Elizabeth Gonzalez Arriba." Address: "Casa Número 4 de San Felipe La Vista, Antigua, Guatemala."

"Of course," Judy remembers. "Cassandra is Clayton's wife, and that must be the address of Hogar Nuevo Día. Cassandra was the one who told me that Ellie had two rowdy, misbehaving brothers who arrived with her the day they dropped her off."

Judy and I are both sleuths now, and our emotions hinge on every word in these seemingly ancient papers.

In my notes, I record Antonia's social situation spelled out before us:

She was interned in Hogar Nuevo Día para Niños. July 21, 1999 . . . Juana Antonia gave up her child due to her poor economic situation . . . She had no way to support her in El Salvador . . . At the same time renounces her rights over child . . . Mother of child presents a troublesome and conflicted personality that makes her interpersonal relationships difficult . . . Furthermore she tends to be aggressive, presented psychosomatic symptoms and suffers from extremely low self-esteem . . . October 21, 1999: Juana Antonia appeared again before the court and stated that upon reflecting on the matter preferred that her daughter be put up for adoption . . . Stated that previous efforts to recover the girl were stated as a weak and selfish moment . . . Finally said she'll go to El Salvador soon with no intention of returning . . . November 23, 1999, court of Escuintla files.

Two things stand out in this document: one is obvious and, I think, alarming, while the other is much more subtle. First of all, it appears that Antonia tried to *reclaim* Ellie three months after giving her up—and eighteen days after her daughter's eighth birthday. My God, I can't imagine the pain she must have been going through. Worse yet, in terms of us finding her, she apparently returned to El Salvador with no intention of returning. How are we ever going to find her if she's in another country altogether, and who knows where?

I reread the dossier on my lap, and the word *Tiquisate*, in the department of Escuintla, appears twice. Judy and I climb the stairs and return to the kitchen, where Bob produces a world atlas, already open to the page with a map of Central America. First I scan the sliver of a country that is El Salvador for any sight of Tiquisate or Escuintla. Nada. There is a district of Escuintla in Guatemala, however, just south of Antigua and Guatemala City and extending down to the Pacific coast. The capital of the district is the port of Escuintla, the third-largest city in the country. I study the map for a good thirty seconds before, there, the word *Tiquisate* jumps out at me—a town west of Escuintla, a little way south of the coastal highway and about thirty kilometers north of the Pacific itself.

"It looks like the coastal lowlands," I tell Judy and Bob. "If that's where Ellie is from, she might remember sugarcane, or bananas, or something like that."

"But Ellie says she's Salvadoran." Judy holds her ground.

"I know, it's confusing," I say. "But the paperwork suggests she's Guatemalan, and her birth certificate has her born in Tiquisate, not Quitisate. Is it possible that, as a young girl, her world was so small that she thought she was in El Salvador, especially if Antonia was originally from that country and moved to Guatemala at some point?"

Judy gives me a blank stare. She's clearly more inclined to believe her daughter than she is some dusty old document that, I admit, could be forged. As for me, I don't know what to believe.

⟡

Less than a month later I'm in Antigua, walking into the Radisson Hotel south of town, on a tip from an American social worker I met at the Marriott in Guatemala City who used to work for Clayton and Cassandra at Hogar Nuevo Día but has since had a falling-out with them. Their driver picks up couples at the Radisson who are there to adopt and takes them to the orphanage to meet the kids, she told me. But the receptionist at the hotel claims she's never heard of a Hogar Nuevo Día and doesn't seem very willing to help me. I leave the Radisson's fancy lobby feeling defeated, but then I remember another thing the social worker told me: walk down the road away from the Radisson about a mile until you see the heavily guarded entrance of a ranch, which she told me is owned by Guatemala's president . . . Hogar Nuevo Día is near there.

The problem is that I don't know which direction to walk. To the right, about fifty yards away, begin the cobblestone streets of downtown Antigua. I know there aren't any ranches in that direction. So I turn left and walk past a gas station and down a lonely road away from Antigua, with garbage littering the gutters on both sides of the road and mud puddles everywhere. This is September, the height of the rainy season in Guatemala, and I'd like to get back to town before the afternoon when the torrents will begin.

I walk for about ten minutes, passing a giant Nestlé industrial plant with trucks entering and leaving and exchanging the obligatory "Buenos días" with the few people I meet. I have to remain alert to avoid the road's numerous potholes and jump out of the way of passing chicken buses lest they spray mud puddles on me, all the while watching for a ranch of presidential proportions.

After a while I come across a Mayan woman and her daughter pushing a vegetable cart down a dirt path perpendicular to the road I'm walking on. "Do you know of a *hogar para niños* near here?" I ask them, using the more common term for an orphanage: a "home for children." The daughter blushes and nods, pointing farther down the dirt path and telling me to turn left at the next paved street. "Buena suerte." Good luck, she wishes me.

Their directions lead me to a different *hogar*, called Semillas de Amor, "Seeds of Love." But across the street is a school full of people. I enter and ask a janitor if he knows of Hogar Nuevo Día. I'm beginning to wonder if it really exists.

"Oh, sure," he assures me. "Walk back down the dirt path you just came from, and before you get to the main road, by Arzú's ranch, you'll see a gray brick building under construction and blocked off. That's Hogar Nuevo Día."

Right, the *former* president Alvaro Arzú, I think. That's what the social worker was talking about. And sure enough, back on the corner, shielded from the road by a big tree, is a brick building virtually covered in a layer of tarp. A team of men is working on the roof, building a second level. Yet there are no signs for Hogar Nuevo Día, and I hear no children's voices.

"¿Aquí hay niños?" Are there children here? I ask one of the construction workers. He nods, long and slow, and points to an opening in the tarp where I can enter. Beyond it I find an open courtyard, as many homes in Guatemala have, but this one is in disrepair. No colorful bougainvillea vines hanging from the walls, and there is no fountain spouting water. Neglect, I think. There are two women hanging clothes from a line: tiny baby clothes. I introduce myself and tell them I am a friend of Judy's helping her track down her daughter's biological mother. I leave out the part about writing a book. "Eleanor Patricia" was her name, I say. "She was seven when she came and lived here for a year."

"Oh, yes, I remember the *niña*," one says. My heart skips a beat. "From the Costa Sur, the southern coast." Hmm, I think. That means Tiquisate, here in Guatemala. Or is that just what they've all been told?

"I need to talk to Clayton and Cassandra," I continue. "Are they here?"

"No, Don Clayton and Doña Cassandra moved to Miami," they answer. "But we can give you the phone number for Hogar Nuevo Día's office where the files are kept."

I'm elated—just a few hours of sleuthing, and I've as good as tracked her down. I call the office, and the receptionist tells me she has no record of a child by that name adopted five years ago, or maybe she just won't share it with me. No, she isn't willing to give me Clayton's phone number in Miami, either, even though she confirms that he still runs the orphanage from afar.

I slam down my cellular phone in frustration. What is going on with this orphanage? Do they have something to hide? No Internet listing, no number in a Guatemalan phone book, not even a sign on the outside of the building. And no help from the stubborn receptionist at the office, either. That evening I search for the name Clayton Phelpers in Florida on WhitePages.com and find four listings. I call all four, and each one denies that he runs an orphanage in Guatemala.

By now I am absolutely convinced that Hogar Nuevo Día has forged Ellie's paperwork to make her easier to adopt, and I figure that Antonia must be in El Salvador. At least I know her name, I think. Well, if even that's real. So I ask the Salvadoran owner of a restaurant I know in Antigua if his country has any kind of civil registry where I could find out where someone lives.

"The government has an online voting registry that they used in the last election," he tells me. "But it's doubtful that a poor, illiterate prostitute actually voted."

Nevertheless, I send a query to a Web site called ElSalvador.com, and wait anxiously for a response. When no answer arrives for twenty-four hours, I decide to make a trip to the southern coast, to Tiquisate, not really expecting it to yield much.

ᘒ

The chicken-bus drivers waiting in the terminal behind Antigua's crowded market honk their horns and yell out the name of their destination with the repetition of auctioneers until they decide that enough passengers have climbed aboard, and then they start their motors and drive down the cobblestone Alameda Santa Lucia, looking for more people to squeeze three to a seat, all the while belching out exhaust on anyone unlucky enough to be standing nearby. The bus to Escuintla then veers south, passing the Radisson, Hogar Nuevo Día and Arzú's ranch, until Volcán de Agua rises up on the left. I am sitting toward the front, on the left-hand side of the bus, so that I can catch a glimpse of the orphanage under construction as we roll by.

All I have with me is a notebook with Antonia's full name and Ellie's birth information written on the first page and a wad of a few hundred quetzales stuffed in my pocket. No camera, no wallet, no passport. I am going to the Costa Sur, a hot and often red-blooded climate where I will stick out as the only gringo for miles. If I get robbed or pickpocketed, I figure they won't get much.

And that's just what happens an hour later when I am jumping off one chicken bus and climbing onto another in the middle of Escuintla. When we arrive at the intersection of the Pacific highway running west toward my destination, the next bus is already rolling forward and pick-ing up speed, so I sprint toward it and pull myself up through the rear emergency door that the ticket collector has opened for me. Buses rarely make complete stops for new passengers in this country. For just a moment I stand on the ladder, hanging off the back of the bus waiting to duck inside, and that's ample time for a pickpocket behind me with agile hands to steal the wad of money in my left pocket. I don't actually feel his hand, but I discover a moment later that my money is gone.

Darn. How will I get to Tiquisate and back again now that I am completely broke? I still have an hour or two of travel time ahead of me, and I begin to doubt whether this is all worth it. Maybe Ellie *was* born in Tiquisate, and so what? I'm not going to find Antonia there . . . she returned to El Salvador years ago, as the dossier said, and by now she's probably dead.

Out of nowhere I hear a voice in clear American English. "Hey, man, what's happening?" I look across the aisle, and, lo and behold, I am not alone. Along one of the stretches of Guatemalan highway that sees the fewest foreigners, I strike up a conversation with Aldo, an Italian American medical student traveling to a tiny town to volunteer at a rural clinic for the next eight months. Because he is a countryman and here to help the poor, I am more than eager to share my mission with Aldo, whom I trust, and before he disembarks he slips me a hundred quetzales (about thirteen dollars). My karma is improving, I hope, and I'll need it today.

"Sale para Tiquisate." Exit for Tiquisate, the ticket collector yells at me in his guttural voice, and I jump off the bus onto a steamy highway next to a roadside food stand where the ladies keeping cool under a dark canopy stare at me as if I had two heads.

"¿Donde está el camino para Tiquisate?" Where is the road for Tiquisate? I ask, realizing that there's nothing I can do today to maintain a low profile.

Three arms rise in unison and point me toward a street branching off to the left, where a half-dozen men in shorts and sandals wait under a makeshift bus shelter, the sun beating down mercilessly on them.

"¿Eres cristiano?" Are you a Christian? one man asks me when I join them at the bus stop. I think for a moment and answer in the affirmative. Of course, there are foreign missionaries all over this country, and the locals are so used to them they don't feel threatened. Better to be disseminating the word of God than to be investigating a woman who gave up her kid for adoption years ago. I make a mental note to bring a Bible along next time.

But when we get on the bus for Tiquisate, a forty-five-minute journey through sugarcane and fruit plantations, a man whom I recognize from the last bus sits down next to me and asks what my real purpose in Tiquisate is. Before I can answer, he pronounces those four syllables that have struck fear into the hearts of so many Guatemalan women: "A-dop-ci-ón . . . ¿Buscas a una mujer que dejó su niña en adopción?" Are you looking for a woman who gave up her child to adoption? Oh, no! My inner alarm goes off. He must have overhead my conversation with Aldo and understood enough English to follow along.

"Maybe I can help you," says the man, too large to be a *campesino* peasant working in the fields. A smile spreads across his face, and he extends his right hand to greet me. "Raúl Capollo es mi nombre. Para servirle."

I should be worried now. I've spent enough time in Guatemala to know that you can't trust just anybody when it comes to a sensitive issue like adoption. What if there is a human-trafficking ring that smuggles babies from the southern coast to Guatemala City to sell them to American couples? What if Raúl Capollo is part of that industry?

Ah, what the heck, another voice in my head counters. I need all the help I can get in finding Antonia. This Raúl already knows what I am doing here, and he might know her. I just won't tell him that I am writing a book about adoption.

"Mucho gusto, Raúl," I answer. "That's right. The woman I am looking for gave up her child about six years ago. I am a friend of the family in *El Norte* that adopted her, and we want to know if she is still alive. The problem is that we think she is Salvadoran, and she might have returned to that country afterwards."

"What is her profession?" Raúl asks.

"We think she is a prostitute."

"Ay, *Dios mío*. There are a lot of Salvadoran prostitutes here. They come here to find work. Their country is even poorer than ours."

A long pause ensues. I pull down the window to let in some fresh air. It's hot here.

"You know the birth name of the *niña*, right?" Raúl continues.

I nod.

"Then why don't you get off at the Hospital Nacional just before the town and ask if they have any record of the girl and if they have an address for the mother?" I make note of the fact that Raúl doesn't ask me for anyone's name. His intentions must be sound.

"If they can't help you, then go to the Municipalidad in Tiquisate and talk to my friend Gerónimo Mendez. '*Chomo*,' we call him. He's the public record keeper, and he might be able to help you. Tell him Raúl sent you."

Obediently, I write down the name "Gerónimo Mendez," and thank Raúl, who ushers me off the bus a moment later when a big modern building behind a security gate appears on the right.

"Here is the hospital," he tells me. "Good luck."

Outside the gate, a dozen locals, mostly women and children, wait to enter. But I meet the security guard's eyes, and he asks me what I need.

"The maternity ward," I say, trying to sound as official as possible. "I have a meeting with the director of the maternity ward." And just as if I'd simply snapped my fingers, the gate opens about three feet, and I walk inside.

I wait for about twenty minutes on a comfortable chair inside an air-conditioned lobby and drink purified water from a Styrofoam cup that a nurse named Lucia kindly gives me. Just before Melanie, the maternity ward director, invites me to enter her office and pull up a chair, it occurs to me to ask Lucia if she remembers a fire in a hotel here in Tiquisate sometime during the mid-1990s. A shrug, Lucia hasn't lived in town that long.

"The girl you are inquiring about, Eleanor Patricia Beneníce Ortiz, was born here," Melanie confirms. "Yes, that's right. October 3, 1991, at 9:15 a.m." Just like in the dossier Judy showed me. My scalp begins to tingle, and I lean in closer for the key question.

"Señora, I really appreciate your help. But I was wondering if you could lend me a hand in finding the birth mother, Juana Antonia

Cubillas Rodrigues. If she's still here in Tiquisate, I'd like to meet her."

"Well, we do have an address registered for the woman when she gave birth to the girl. But I'm afraid I can't just give that to you. I'll need some kind of permission from the mother who adopted the child. She'll have to fax it to us, authorizing me to give you the address. You understand."

I look toward the floor, feeling defeated. Today I had hoped to at least determine whether Antonia was still in Tiquisate . . . and now the endless bureaucracy begins.

"Anyhow," Melanie adds, "if Antonia was a poor Salvadoran sex worker, as you say, then I'm sure the address she gave us was false. Many of these women are just passing through town, and they just scribble something down in the margin."

I thank Melanie and promise that she'll receive a fax within a couple days from Judy Barrett, even though in my mind I don't think there's any reason to go to the trouble. The director is right. The address they have from 1991 is probably just bogus.

On the way out the door of the hospital I fight through my frustration to thank the nurse named Lucia.

"Oh, just one thing," she calls after me. "I asked a colleague who has worked here longer than I have about your question. She says there was a fire in Tiquisate, around the year 1993. But it wasn't a hotel; it was here in the hospital. In fact, this is a brand-new hospital. The old one burned down. She said there was some kind of fireworks accident."

❧

The midday sun has reached the top of the sky by the time I walk out through the hospital's gates and onto the street again, and in my anxious condition I'm not ready to handle the intense heat. So I hail one of the three-wheeled taxies called a Tuc-tuc for two and a half quetzales (about thirty-three cents) and ask the driver to take me to the Municipalidad, the town hall in Tiquisate, where all official business here happens. This is my last chance at finding an address for Antonia, today at least, and I know it. I cross my fingers, hoping that Raúl's friend "Chomo" can work miracles.

Tiquisate is basically just one main street that, according to the map, continues south toward the Pacific Ocean after the town ends. Rutted dirt paths jut off from both sides, and small-town Central American life happens everywhere in the form of women standing outside their *tiendas* blaring merengue music, most of them dressed in thin T-shirts, sandals, and short shorts, almost provocative. Prostitutes? I wonder. No, it's just damn hot here in the Costa Sur. This part of Guatemala feels much more Caribbean than the chilly Mayan highlands, and I wonder if that automatically means sexual promiscuity. Boys on bicycles hoot and holler when they pass by *chicas* walking on the side of the road, revealing much of their thighs, and sometimes even breast cleavage.

We pass the traditional market on the left side of the street where vendors are selling fresh fruits and vegetables, tortillas, meats, and clothing under their tin sheet roofs, this all right next to the terminal where buses honk their horns in preparation for trips to Escuintla, Mazatenango farther to the west, and even directly to Guatemala City. What I notice right away about Tiquisate is that there is no one dressed in indigenous clothing or speaking any of the twenty-two Mayan languages, even though the people are clearly descendants of that great empire. The colorful *trajes* and *huipiles* worn by the women are confined to the volcanoes and *altiplano* to the north and west, where ancient traditions are preserved, where a greater sense of community prevails, and where, I figure, the subject of giving up children ultimately to foreigners is taboo.

Just after the Telgua telecom station at the southern end of town where I begin to see more dusty empty lots than I do open businesses, the Tuc-tuc turns right and stops in front of a two-story concrete building painted with what looks like a new coat of orange: the town hall. True to Central America, a line of people waits under the building's eaves near a teller's window. They are shielded from the vicious sun, but sweat still pours down their foreheads. And just like those waiting in front of the gate to the hospital, all eyes quickly focus on me, and the teller asks how he can help me (before anyone else).

"Gerónimo Mendez. I'm here to see el Señor Gerónimo Mendez."

"Pas adelante." Right this way. The preferential treatment awaits me, as always. A security guard opens the door and lowers his shotgun so that I can enter. A secretary opens a second door and, with a smile, ushers me into an office full of desks overflowing with papers and people running about the room in no particular pattern that I can discern. Against each of the walls are six-foot-high shelves of huge books and binders, and for a moment I feel as if I've entered an ancient library.

Suddenly the commotion stops, and the people on their feet, who I figure are secretaries and bookkeepers, move off to the left or right, opening a line of sight between me and an old man with shining silvery hair elegantly combed to the right and wearing a clean white short-sleeved shirt with blue stripes, unbuttoned at the top. He sits behind a grand wooden desk, which I realize now is the center of the office, gripping a ballpoint pen between the thumb and forefinger of his right hand with a mountain of papers waiting to be signed. But when he looks up and sees me, a broad smile spreads across his face. This dignified character must be . . .

"Gerónimo Mendez, aquí para servirle." Here to serve you.

The record keeper of Tiquisate must be as enthralled by my presence as I am by his. Sitting down in a chair in front of his desk, I introduce myself as an American journalist and joke that I'm probably the first one he's seen this week. Gerónimo tosses back his head and chuckles. Then I tell him exactly why I'm here.

"A *Salvadoreña* who gave birth to a little girl here almost fourteen years ago and then gave her up." He ponders the dilemma. "*Pobrecita* . . . if I had ten quetzales for every time that's happened. How's the girl doing now?"

"She's great," I answer, realizing that Gerónimo is the first Guatemalan I've met who has actually asked about the child's current well-being. "She lives with a very kind family in a beautiful part of the country and goes to a very good school. She is a talented artist and musician."

The broad smile returns to his face.

"Así es en El Norte." That's how it is in the United States, Gerónimo says.

"We'll look for a record of the girl's birth. But you said that the mother is not from here. What about the father? Do you know his full name?"

I finish copying the names "Eleanor Patricia Beren**í**ce Ortiz" and "Juana Antonia Cubillas Rodrigues" on a pad of paper, and then look back in my notes for the father, about whom I had almost completely forgotten: "Esvin Arnoldo Ortiz Gonzalez."

Gerónimo hands the pad to one of his assistants, a pretty teenage girl who, with the help of her colleagues, climbs a stepladder and retrieves what looks like a two-foot-high, twenty-pound volume and lowers it down to another girl standing next to the official's desk. The first girl opens the book and carefully unwraps its yellowing pages, which look as brittle as autumn leaves on the forest floor. Then she blows a cloud of dust off the book's open surface and begins studying its contents.

My mouth agape at what's happening before me, I watch as the brain trust of Tiquisate takes a journey into the town's past: to the time before the fire in the hospital and before Guatemala's peace accords were signed. On October 3, 1991, the day Ellie was born, this country was still at war with itself, with guerrilla fighters hiding out in the mountains in the western highlands or escaping to Mexico to kill time until peace could be secured and the army ordered to destroy the enemy before that happened.

The girl looks up from the book. "It's not here," she says, surprised. "We have no record of Eleanor Patricia Beren**í**ce Ortiz being born in Tiquisate."

"Que extraño." How strange, Gerónimo exclaims. "You said that they do have proof of her birth in the hospital?"

I nod.

"Let's look for the father, Esvin Arnoldo. If he really is from Tiquisate, then we'll have a record of his *cedula*."

Of course, I think. His identification papers filed when he was eighteen. They'll have an address for him or his parents.

While the assistant ascends the ladder again to retrieve a different book, Gerónimo leans over the desk and begs me to come closer.

"Why is it that gringos come to this country to adopt our children?" he asks me in a hushed tone so that no one around us can hear our conversation. "I understand that some of them can't have their own, but why here?"

The girl returns with another seemingly ancient book, and Gerónimo quickly whispers to me, "The traffickers are here in town: they're all around us. The lawyers from the capital have come to me and offered to pay me if I'll supply them with a list of illiterate and poor women here in Tiquisate who have more children than they can handle . . . ," before he leans back in his chair and puts his charming smile back on.

Another pair of yellowing pages opens to the light of day for the first time in years, and once again the helper blows away dust so that she can read their content.

"Esvin Arnoldo Ortiz Gonzalez," she reads. "*Cedula* filed in 1987 when he was eighteen years old, living at the address of his parents: Zona 1, 3. Avenida, 3. Calle, 4-6, Tiquisate."

"*Así es.* We've got a match," Gerónimo beams. "His profession is listed here as a mechanic, so if you have trouble finding the address, look for a mechanic and ask him if he knows Esvin."

Of course, who knows if he or his parents still live there? But at least I have a shot in the dark now. I don't really want to meet this Esvin character, the guy who abandoned his family for another woman and, for all I know, could be a violent gun-happy drunk. Nevertheless, this is all I have to go on. Maybe he can tell me if she's still in town or if she returned to El Salvador.

I thank Gerónimo Mendez and his helpers and insist that I'll return soon to hear his tales about adoption, and I show them my right hand with fingers crossed to indicate that I'll still need a lot of luck before I find Antonia.

※

I was clearly fooled by the mention of an *avenida* and a *calle* in the address where I now find myself heading in another three-wheeler Tuc-tuc taxi. There are no avenues or streets in Tiquisate with the exception of the main road heading south to the Pacific. What we are throt-tling down at breakneck speed is nothing more than a dirt path, with potholes, piles of burning plastic garbage, and sleeping dogs forming a daunting obstacle course. When I ask my driver if he can find the corner of 3. Avenida y 3. Calle, he just nods and mumbles, which is more than I can manage because I don't see street signs anywhere.

After about fifteen minutes of what feels like a roller-coaster ride, the taxi driver tells me we are close to that street corner, but that he doesn't know exactly where it is. The shanty houses all around us are crumbling, and they reveal no clues. But twenty yards away I do see a huge truck being worked over by several mechanics as teenage boys load bananas into its trailer. So I thank the driver for his help, and ask him how to get back to the main road. "It's just three blocks straight that way," he assures me, and when I look I do see cars whizzing by, which means I'm not that far out in the boonies.

Gazing around me, I wonder if I'm taking in Ellie's old stomping grounds. Off in the distance, from the direction we just came, is a little *tienda* with women sitting out front waiting for customers. Could that be the place where Ellie remembers going for sweets?

I walk toward the banana truck, which I think is on the corner of 3. Avenida y 3. Calle, and can't help but notice that with me here, a five-foot-nine gringo with short blond hair and blue eyes, wearing white slacks and a white short-sleeved shirt, everything around me is changing. Eyes home in on me. Children stop playing and yelling and just stare. Even the mangy dogs act differently when a foreigner comes around. As the anthropologist would say, I am manipulating my environment.

Almost there now, I tell myself as I take long, deep breaths to keep calm. At any moment I could run into the characters from Ellie's past.

Off to the right of the road, in front of a fading white wall, is a pathetic-looking old man in a wheelchair who is missing both his legs and thrusts the dull machete he holds in his right hand into the ground over and over again, as if he wants it to stick but can't make it do so. Hopefully, he's the most threatening person I'll meet today, I joke to myself.

And then, for some reason, still a block away from the truck, I stop, turn to the left, and out of a one-story brick house walks a little man with a five o'clock shadow and dirty glasses, his right arm in a sling. With his left, he waves at me. Well, this is as good as anyone, I think.

"Excuse me, I'm looking for a mechanic named Esvin Arnoldo. I have work for him. Do you know him?"

Before the man can answer, a teenage boy creeps up next to him and answers me: "Oh, Esvin, he's off getting drunk again," and lifts his hand to his mouth as if he were tipping back a bottle.

The kid is wearing soccer warm-ups, a clean white T-shirt, and running shoes. He doesn't look nearly as poor as everyone else around him. So I introduce myself and ask him how things are going today.

"I just got back from my team's *fútbol* match. We lost today, though."

I rationalize this in my head. An athlete . . . That means, in Guatemala, he's much less likely to be a gang member, or a drug dealer, or someone who'd like to shoot off my head. This kid uses his testosterone on the field. So I go for a goal.

"I'm actually looking for Esvin's ex-wife or former girlfriend from many years ago. Her name is Antonia, and I think she's originally from El Salvador."

The man with his arm in the sling says nothing, but after a moment of silence the young soccer player replies: "Yeah, I know her. She's a *gordita* now, a fat woman. I haven't seen her in a while, but her kids still come and play at their grandparents' house across the street from us."

I just about jump a foot high. "Wait, you say she's here, in Tiquisate? I thought she had returned to El Salvador. How long has it been since you saw her last: days, months, years?"

"Days, no more. I think I saw her last week in the marketplace. Yeah, she goes to visit her mom in El Salvador sometimes, but she still lives here. With another man, on the other side of town."

Barely able to control my emotions now, and knowing I shouldn't reveal too much, I ask about the kids.

"The two *chicos*? Maynor and William. They live with Antonia, but sometimes they come and stay here with Esvin's parents."

The questions pour out of me: Are they doing all right? Are they in school? Working? In gangs? Fathers?

"No, they're not in any trouble. There isn't really any gang activity here in Tiquisate. It's too poor; there's nothing to fight over. They're not in school. But the older one, Maynor, attends the Evangelical church. He's got a girlfriend, and he doesn't drink or smoke or anything."

"What about a girl? Don't they have a sister?" Now I'm putting the kid to the test. What does *he* think happened to Ellie?

"*Pues*, I don't remember any sister. Well, wait, there was one years ago, but she's back in El Salvador, or she died. Who knows?"

And with that I tell my newfound friend, Jaime Sanchez Rodriguez Jr., that Ellie is fine and well in the United States, and that her new mother wants to meet her old mother. Soon, very soon.

"Yeah, sure, I can take you to her. I'd be happy to."

We exchange telephone numbers, and in my excitement, I accidentally shake the right hand of Jaime Sanchez Rodriguez Sr.—the broken one.

The father laughs it off. "*No hay problema, amigo.* Welcome to Tiquisate. Jaime Sanchez Sr. and Jr. are here to serve you. I nicknamed my boy 'Jimmy Carter' because he's such a good diplomat!"

Miracle workers, I think. Between Raúl on the bus, Gerónimo at the Municipalidad, and this father and son tandem, something special has happened today. But I dare not stick around too long, lest I spoil the party. And I don't want to meet Antonia just yet. There's someone I need to tell first.

ॐ

For the first time ever, I don't mind the tossing and turning the Guatemalan chicken bus inflicts on me when it clonks down the highway. That's because I don't even feel it. I am floating on cloud nine.

I have to wait until the bus arrives in Escuintla, though, before I pick up enough of a cellular phone signal to call Judy Barrett, who is otherwise enjoying an insignificant, relaxing fall evening in Traverse City. By the time she picks up the phone, the rain is falling down hard on the sheet-metal roof over my head as I wait at the bus stop for a ride to Antigua, and I almost have to yell to be heard: "I found her, Judy . . . I know where Antonia is!"

A long, long silence follows that feels more like days, even years. I look out at the wet road and see the reflection of the golden arches on the pavement. There is a McDonald's just on the other side of the street. And northern Michigan might as well be here, right now. So might the entire United States, colliding with Guatemala.

Judy can't believe it. She has very few words for this moment. Yet, four days later, she hops on a plane for Guatemala City, rerouted through Mexico after Hurricane Rita slams into Houston.

No matter. The hurricane season won't stop her from meeting the woman who gave birth to her daughter Ellie.

8 ❧ The Meeting

At 6:30 a.m. on Monday, September 26, Judy Barrett knocks on the door of my room at the Motel Texas in Escuintla. She admits it's early, and apologizes for it before even wishing me a good morning, but she's anxious and ready to get going. In reality, so am I, even though I'm not a morning person. This is the day we've both been anticipating for a long time.

"Months after we adopted Ellie we'd still hear her pounding the pillow at night and crying," Judy tells me as we sit down at a plastic table near the motel pool to order breakfast. "Crying because she couldn't understand why her mother abandoned her."

The reflection of morning light off the chlorinated water below mesmerizes us, and a twinkle of dew on the top of the blue plastic waterslide on the other side of the pool catches my eye. A good luck charm?

"She adjusted well, and spoke pretty good English after just six months, but even at Christmastime Ellie always seemed a little distant. 'Who knows what happened to my mom and brothers?' she'd think out loud. 'They're probably dead.'"

"My little girl has a hole in her heart, a hole in her life," Judy continues. "I hope that by coming here and, hopefully, finding her birth mother, I can fill that hole, or at least help her live with it."

Her words are emblematic of a new generation of adoptive parents. Parents who are open to contact with the biological parents, and some who even embrace "open adoptions," in which a line of communication exists between the biological and adoptive parents, before the child even takes his or her first steps. What makes Ellie's case so unique is that it's not the adoptee searching for the birth mother but Judy, without the knowledge of her daughter, yet for her benefit. Whether Judy's calculated decision to go behind Ellie's back is warranted, just, and wise is a good question. As documentarian, and out of respect for this educated and capable adult, I don't share any misgivings I may have.

Betty Jean Lifton believes that reunions are generally a good thing for adopted children from any country, even though problems may arise when the adoptee has access once again to those who relinquished her, especially if there was abuse, or if a relationship of dependency arises between the biological and adoptive families.

The coffee arrives at our table, weak as it usually is in most Guatemalan restaurants that cater mostly to its own citizens, even though the Motel Texas resembles any carport dive off the exit ramp of an American expressway. In particular, the pastel-colored waterslide and plastic tables next to the pool, as well as the greasy fast-food-style menu and the odd vagabond characters always passing through the office, remind me of places off I-75 where my family used to stay on the long drive from Michigan to Florida for spring break.

Two brown-skinned African guys walk by our table, bantering in broken English. Ethiopians, they tell me. What on earth are they doing here in Guatemala? Business, one says with a wink. I don't ask any more questions. We are in Escuintla, a large industrial city near the Pacific coast, and who knows what kinds of products, and what kind of people, pass through this port town, which seems to have an ominous reputation around Guatemala. Besides, Judy and I already have our hands full with our own clandestine mission.

We decide against taking a chicken bus to Tiquisate, an hour and a half away, because we want to make our visit as discreet as possible, and if anything sketchy goes down we'll need to be able to get out of there, fast. So I dicker with the motel staff and convince them to book a private taxi for three hundred quetzales, about forty dollars. That's a lot here, but the driver certainly won't find any passengers there who will pay that kind of money to come all the way back to Escuintla.

Because of the early hour, the desk clerk has to make four calls before she locates a taxi driver willing to take us that far, and when Francisco pulls up outside the motel, we see why. Every part of his vehicle is falling apart. Only two doors open from the outside, there's virtually no muffler, the seats sink halfway to the pavement, and the car maxes out at about forty miles per hour. Francisco himself looks like he's 150 years old.

"But don't worry," he tells us through a smile missing several teeth. "I have my trusty Bible here on the dashboard, and today we will travel in the hands of the Lord." (The Bible looks older and more worn than the car and the man combined.)

Judy and I don't feel very reassured.

I hop into the passenger's seat, returning the Bible to the dashboard each time it falls onto my lap, and Judy sits in the back, though leaning forward through the front seats so that we can talk over the roar of the ancient automobile's motor. Francisco sticks to the right lane at his snail-like pace, and chicken buses and cars, even semis, pass us every few seconds on the Pacific highway.

Judy's nervous, she tells me. We could be putting this woman at risk by showing up out of the blue and telling her about Ellie. She may never want to think again about the seven-year-old girl she gave up for adoption, and this might open painful wounds in her. Worse yet, maybe her other kids and family don't know she gave Ellie up, and they'll be furious with her once they find out. There's another man in her life, the younger Jaime told me when I was in Tiquisate five days ago. And how will he react to our presence? Will he be jealous? Will he hurt Antonia? Many women who relinquish their children, both in the United States and abroad, don't tell their future spouses and children. Instead, like Norma from the coffee *fincas*, they bury the secret. Subsequently, many adoption reunions have been impeded by the biological mother's refusal to admit to her current family that the person knocking on their door is actually her own—out of shame or out of fear. Equally important, will we compromise our own safety by barging into this village? Is there a better, more discreet way to meet Antonia for the first time?

We need to find a neutral setting where she can come and meet us, Judy decides. We know about a place called the Hotel Familiar, which the travel agent in the Guatemala City airport recommended to us when Judy arrived yesterday. Hopefully, Jaime can go and bring her to us. If we go directly to Antonia's home, unannounced, the results could be disastrous. "We need to respect her," Judy repeats like a mantra.

Off to the right looms Volcán de Fuego, the Volcano of Fire, which is more familiar from the north side, from Antigua—the safety of Antigua.

"How many people in Tiquisate know about us already?" Judy asks into my left ear. The tone of her voice suggests how nervous she is. With a question like that, she can't help but put me on the spot even though she doesn't mean to be condescending.

"Jaime Jr. and Jaime Sr., who I think are Ellie's birth father's neighbors. I told them not to let anyone else know. Plus the guy in the municipality who helped me out, and the girls working for him who found the address that led me to the Jaimes. There are also the women at the hospital where Ellie was born. Oh, yeah, and the guy on the chicken bus named Raúl who recommended that I go to the municipality. But no one except the Jaimes know who Antonia is."

"Are there any other ways of meeting a biological mother that you know of?" Judy asks, betraying second thoughts about what we're doing.

There is an organization called Guatemalan Roots that facilitates reunions between adopted kids and their Guatemalan birth families. Two women, one in Guatemala City and the other in Boston, spend months interviewing both the families in the United States and here, sending videos and letters back and forth before the actual reunion happens, in a *parque central* in some neutral town in Guatemala. It's much more meticulous and thorough than what we are doing today. A reunion facilitated through Guatemalan Roots is the climax of a long, careful process, and it costs the adoptive family several thousand dollars.

"We can still turn back if you want, Judy," I break an awkward silence. "If this doesn't feel right today, we don't need to commit to anything."

"No, no," she says without even a moment's hesitation. "I want to do this, or at least give it our best shot. Bob has plenty of second thoughts about this trip. He's worried about the safety of everyone involved, especially you and me. But I told him we'd be careful. I want to fill the hole in Ellie's heart."

By and by, our driver, Francisco, reaches Rio Bravo and turns left, off the Pacific highway and toward Tiquisate, a mere eight kilometers away.

ॐ

At 10:00 a.m. we arrive in Tiquisate, and the air is so hot and steamy it almost casts mirages in front of us. Francisco doesn't know the purpose of our trip here, but he drives as if he is nervous anyway, hardly touching the gas pedal and pulling over to let even bicycles and Tuc-tuc taxis pass us, before I tell him to speed up, the Hotel Familiar is on the other side of town, according to the signs, and we're not going to miss it.

We pass the Pollo Ranchero fried chicken restaurant three blocks from where the Jaimes live, and then the central market and the bus terminal. Judy is staring out the window, awestruck, or maybe horrified, by the people loitering up and down the main street. Grinding poverty, confusion, absolute boredom in their faces, as they have nowhere to go and nothing to do. And the kicker: Antonia could be any one of these middle-aged women. Ellie's past is all around us.

Opposite the municipal building we turn down a dirt road leading us toward the hotel and bounce about fifty yards over potholes and ruts. Nice and discreet, I think: off the beaten path. The people of Tiquisate will soon see two gringos walking around, and then tell all their friends and neighbors, but we can hop a Tuc-tuc and return to the hotel, and they won't know where we've gone.

Judy is one step ahead of me by the time we arrive at the hotel office. "Let's just get one room for now," she suggests, "just in case we don't want to stay here tonight. And let's use anonymous names." And so "Julia," a short middle-aged woman with a blue-collar southeastern Michigan accent and a Spanish-speaking young man named "Geoffrey" with a slight tan and a notebook in hand sign their names in the guest book of the Hotel Familiar and pay for one room, with the possibility of another one later on today. The manager, a clean-shaven man in his late twenties, originally from Guatemala City and with a western air of hospitality about him, must be thinking . . . "How strange."

But entertaining foreign guests is a rare and welcome opportunity, so he offers to drive Julia and Geoffrey around town in his pickup and point out whatever they want to see, though he can't imagine what that would be.

"Tiquisate is pretty safe," he tells me. "Not much goes on here. No gangs, no assaults on tourists [what tourists?], just poverty." Two minutes later, he drops us off at the market, having shown us the whole town. Judy has her camera out and wants to shoot pictures of the market and the bus terminal, something for Ellie to see and remember just in case we have to leave here in a hurry.

And this is when the stares begin. All around us, people stop walking, stop slapping tortillas, stop honking, stop fixing mopeds, stop flirting with girls in miniskirts, and ten thousand eyes descend on us. Gringos—what on earth are they doing here? But to me, they don't feel like threatening stares, just curious stares. These people aren't going to rob us or beg us for money. They have no practice with such skills, because on any normal day in Tiquisate, there's no one to beg for money. So for the moment we are safe.

The camera clicks a sixth time. "Okay, that's enough for now," Judy declares. "Everyone is watching us." And so we walk four blocks to the Pollo Ranchero, and before turning down the dirt path to confront the heady moment of first contact, we duck into a *tienda* for a couple of bottles of Orange Crush to help calm our nerves. But the shopkeeper won't let us walk out of her store with perfectly good glass bottles. Anything solid is worth money in these parts. So we leave Judy's pink handbag as collateral, promising we'll be back within the half hour. Reluctantly, she accepts.

❦

The legless old man in the wheelchair poking the dull machete into the dirt is on the other side of the path this time, but he remembers me from the previous Wednesday, and he welcomes us with a wide, toothless smile as he points his machete toward the house of the Jaimes. Both Senior and Junior come through the gate to meet us, and while I wear a jovial face, Judy is clearly very nervous.

And why shouldn't she be? Less than twenty hours ago she was on an American airplane surrounded by everything familiar, being served pretzels and a beverage by the flight attendant. Here she is now in a tiny impoverished town in the middle of nowhere, being asked to rely on total strangers speaking in a foreign tongue to do her family the ultimate favor: introduce her to Ellie's birth mother.

Pleasantries are exchanged, and Jaime Sr. invites us into their living quarters, a linoleum-floored room with a black-and-white television in the corner and the obligatory painting of Jesu Cristu on the far wall. Junior fetches two plastic chairs for us and begs us to sit while he and his father stand. Hospitality. Sitting in a third chair, watching television, is a darker-skinned, Rastafarian-like kid with dreadlocks, named Mario, whom I haven't met before. But he seems to pay little attention to our conversation, initially at least.

"Muy bonita casa," Judy begins the conversation in a wavering voice that reveals her unrest. Despite her broken Spanish, she insists on playing a role in this investigative game, choosing small talk as her method of entry. "¿Pero que pasó aqui?" What happened here? Judy points to his right arm in the sling. I remind her in English that the father and son already know why we are here, and that they are our best hope to find Antonia. The Rasta kid in the corner, I don't know about, but he's probably harmless.

"¿Cómo esta Antonia?" Judy's face tightens as she jumps right to the heart of the matter, using the name of Ellie's birth mother for what I think is the first time. "¿Recuerdan a Eleanor Patricia?" Do you remember Eleanor Patricia?

Jaime Jr. nods. He is calm and without emotion.

"Un poquito. No mucho." But yes, her brothers Maynor and William still come around here every weekend to visit their grandparents, who live just across the street.

"¿Esvin?" Judy's face cringes when she utters the name of Ellie's inebriated birth father.

"Sí, Esvin's parents. But we don't see him much. He's off with Esperanza, his new woman, drinking."

"Was there another brother named Erik?"

"Yeah, there was, but we haven't seen him in a long time, either. He's probably in El Salvador, or dead."

In contrast to Junior's calm, Jaime Sr. seems uptight and fidgety throughout this conversation. He is standing over us, clenching his right arm, as a look of pain appears in his eyes.

"Does Mario remember Ellie?"

Jaime Sr.'s eyes grow large, and he answers for the Rastafarian, his voice implying urgency: "¡El no sabe nada!" He knows nothing. Senior's left index finger slices through the air as if telling us to stop the questions. Senior turns to Mario and suggests that they leave the room, and as soon as we are alone with Junior, he tells us that Mario is Ellie's cousin, the son of one of Esvin's brothers.

"Oh, no!" Judy and I blurt simultaneously. Now a family member knows already. And not one of Ellie's siblings but a kid related to Esvin, that mean drunk who abandoned his whole family for another woman. Judy tells me she is worried about Mario running off and telling people about our presence. And what if Antonia finds out before we are able to make contact with her? Will it scare her away? Will Esvin's family unleash rage on her for knowing that one of his children is alive and well in *El Norte*? We'll have to make our plan now and then get back to the hotel, we both agree.

I ask Junior for the huge favor: "Go to Antonia's house and bring her to Casa Familiar where we are staying, at high noon, one hour from now. Try to find her before Mario tells anyone else. And tell her that two gringos are here to offer her work . . . nothing about Eleanor Patricia." I tell a white lie, borrowing from the advice of the social worker I met at the Marriott.

"No," Judy interjects. "*La verdad.* Tell her the truth about why we are here."

Jaime Jr. nods his head, studying our every word, seemingly understanding the predicament we are in. I ask if he thinks he can pull it off. Junior responds that the problem might be if Antonia's new man is there with her. He'll want to know why she is leaving, and he'll want to come along.

I ponder this one. We are in a very machismo culture where the men scarcely let their women breathe without permission. Gringos asking Antonia to reveal secrets from her past? That will never fly with her new guy. But Judy grabs me by the arm and ushers me out the door, wary of Mario, and tells me we need to return to the hotel and just hope for the best.

I have time only to slip Junior 10 quetzales (about $1.25)—enough for a few taxi rides, and wish him *buena suerte* (good luck). I catch the worried expression on his face before we reach the dirt path.

On the other side of it is Mario, with his back to us, crouched over an old set of stereo speakers with a screwdriver in hand. Of course, he's a mechanic, just like his uncle. His armless basketball warm-up jersey hangs loose around his chest, showing his chocolate-colored skin. He looks like one of the Garifuna fishermen from Guatemala's Caribbean coast—part Indian, part European, part African former slave. I place my hand on his left shoulder and ask him if he thinks he'll be able to fix the speakers. No answer.

Then I get right to the point, almost pleading with him not to tell anyone about Ellie or our presence here. He just grunts. We walk away, back toward the hotel, not knowing if Mario is harmless or whether he will become our Achilles' heel.

It takes Judy and me twenty minutes to walk back to the Hotel Familiar after leaving our empty bottles at the *tienda* on the corner. We move at a brisk pace because we are nervous, and she asks me for the time almost every other step we take. I try to play the role of eternal optimist. We've set up the reunion and done everything we can, I tell her. Now we'll just have to wait and hope for the best. "Let the cards fall as they may."

The dining room–reception area of the hotel is open when we arrive at 11:30, but they aren't serving lunch yet. To satisfy our hunger and, equally important, to give us a way to pass the time, Judy and I visit another *tienda* next door and stock up on packs of saltine crackers and squares of fresh goat cheese that are very popular in Guatemala.

We take a seat at the second table farthest from the door, under a black-and-white portrait of a happy young Elvis cradling an electric guitar in his arms. On the blue-and-white-checkered tablecloth, Judy spreads out our snack. She gets a knife from the hotel kitchen and slices thin strips of cheese, which she places between two crackers to make minisandwiches for us. Judy is playing the role of mother.

Our taste buds are hypertuned to every flavor, as we are on high alert: the salty residue of the crackers on our lips, the sour bite of the cheese piercing the glands at the corners of our mouths. Every sound, every smell prompts one of us to jump up and look out the window onto the dusty dirt path to see if someone is arriving. At 11:45 the hotel maids enter the kitchen and then leave again. Occasionally a car or a scooter drives by, torturing Judy and me. The manager of the hotel slams the door of his pickup and returns to the reception desk. Outside, a half-dozen little kids hang out in front of the *tienda* where we bought our snack.

I run up to the room to grab my tape recorder and camera, to record the historic encounter, and Judy does the same with her manila envelope of Ellie pictures she has brought for Antonia. What better way to talk about the daughter they share in common than with photos of her?

But high noon comes and goes without a sign. Guatemalans aren't punctual like we are in the United States, of course, but this wait is a killer. The sun glaring through the window is taking its toll on our energy level, and our clothes stick to our bodies like wet laundry. We've been awake for six hours—six very intense hours, and as the minutes tick by, 12:05, 12:06, 12:10, it seems that our quest will have all been for naught. We decide 12:30 will be the cutoff time. I suggest that I'll head back to the Jaimes' place, alone, to find out what happened. But Judy doesn't like that idea. It can only lead to trouble, she says. We'll take naps if they aren't here by 12:30, and then catch a cab back to Escuintla, or farther north to Antigua.

It was an honorable attempt, she tells me, but let's not force anything. Let Antonia have her peace and quiet. The woman's probably suffered enough already. At least we have pictures of Tiquisate to take back and show Ellie. That's enough, right?

❧

At 12:25 the low rumble of a three-wheeled Tuc-tuc taxi's motor wakes me from my daydream. I stick my head out the window, but the little red car has stopped too close to the hotel, and in the shade it is shielded from my view. I tell Judy that I'll go outside and see what's up, and like a jackrabbit I bound out the door.

In the midday glare I can't yet make out any of the people walking toward me. My eyes take five seconds to adjust before I identify Jaime Jr. paying the taxi driver the fare of 2.5 quetzales . . . and there, just a few feet away from me and moving ever closer, is a short and plump woman with a big round face sporting a good-natured smile. She wears a loose-fitting, sleeveless white-and-yellow flowery dress that can't conceal her enormous belly or her chubby legs. And my initial thought, I don't know why, is . . . "This can't be Antonia!" But what was I expecting: a replica of pretty and innocent Ellie, just a couple of decades older?

I extend my right hand and introduce myself and then ask for her name.

"Me llamo Antonia Cubillas Rodriges, señor. Con mucho gusto."
A pleasure to meet you, sir, the woman says in formal Spanish, as if
she were speaking to her boss or a statesman. Her eyes have that illuminated look of happiness as she shakes my hand, and I tell myself
this is a good sign.

I pivot 180 degrees so that I can lead her into the hotel dining
room, and there, in the doorway, frozen stiff and absolutely quiet,
is Judy. Her eyes stare at this woman in front of her who apparently
bore her youngest daughter, studying her as she might a chess set. And
this is the moment when I, the documentarian, the matchmaker, the
translator, have no idea what to do. I move out of the way and let the
story unfold.

Suddenly, Junior's voice enters the scene from somewhere behind
us, uttering the words, "Aquí esta Maynor, su hijo." Here is Maynor,
her son. And out of the midday glare appears Ellie's older brother, a
handsome young man of sixteen with a well-defined face and hands,
though he is of slender build. Maynor's complexion is a bit lighter
than that of his mother, his dark hair is slicked to the left with gel, and
he wears a stylish black Diesel shirt, untucked over his blue jeans. So
this is the kid who played with Ellie in the mudflats, who toughened
her up so she could run with the boys, and who chased after the car
in Antigua those many years ago, trying to stop them from taking
his sister away.

The next thirty seconds are a blur. We all enter the dining room,
the five of us, but there are only four wooden chairs around the table,
so I return to the front of the room to grab another one.

When I return, three bottles of ice-cold Coca-Cola have been
placed before our guests. Judy is seated to my right, already showing
photos of Ellie to Antonia, who is to her right, across the table from
me. Jaime Jr., to my left, sits there in silence, with a puzzled look on
his face. And Maynor, seated between Judy and me, has already placed
his head on the table, shaking and bawling.

I exchange glances with Jaime Jr., seeking advice on how to proceed,
but the serious expression on his face mirrors mine. I ask Antonia if

she minds my recording the ensuing conversation, which she doesn't, so I put the recorder in the middle of the table and then let my human instinct take hold, placing my right hand on Maynor's upper back, and rubbing it for comfort, even though I've known this kid for all of a minute.

Meanwhile, the tape rolls.

"Me sufrí mucho." I suffered a lot with their father, Esvin, Antonia answers Judy, who is trying to glean the factual information from this woman first. "He was a drinker, and he abused me."

"How many kids did you have?"

"Seven kids together with him. Maynor, William, Erik, Cindy Siomara, Cindy Estefania, Alicia, and Bereníce [Ellie]." Antonia holds up her fingers and counts with them, then she pauses. "There were three other kids from different men in El Salvador, where my mother lives."

"Ten kids!" Judy confirms in an incredulous tone.

"Sí, bastante."

"Did Eleanor Patricia grow up here or in El Salvador?" I jump in.

"Who?" Antonia needs clarification.

"Bereníce, he means Bereníce," Jaime answers, realizing that their girl has a different name now.

"Oh, *la niña*. She spent most of her time here, but sometimes we would visit my mother in El Salvador, when there was money to travel. Sometimes for fifteen days, or a few months at a time."

"That's interesting, because Ellie has always thought of herself as Salvadoran," Judy says, puzzled.

"What ever happened to their father?"

"He kicked me out of the house. He found another woman, named Esperanza."

"Ellie remembers this too," says Judy, her upper body tilted toward Antonia and her face concentrating on every word.

"I was pregnant at the time." Antonia's voice cracks. "He kicked me out, said the house was his. But I paid to have that house built with my own money that I earned. *Me sufrí mu-ucho.*" Antonia draws out her vowels when she recounts her tales of woe.

"And how about Maynor? What is he doing these days?" The boy's head rises from the table, his eyes still wet with tears, though a look of contentment has come over his face. Is he thinking about his sister, visualizing meeting her again?

Maynor doesn't have work, Antonia explains. He dropped out of school years ago after completing the third grade, around the same time Ellie stopped going. There was no money to pay for tuition or books. Now he attends the Evangelical church in town, and that is where he met his girlfriend, Guadalupe. Antonia and the boys live with her boyfriend, Wagner, in a place they rent near the market.

Judy leans forward, her voice climbs an octave, and she steers the conversation in a new direction. "Ellie remembers so much . . . like the market," as if she is trying to bring her daughter's presence here to this place. "Ellie esta feliz ahora, pero corazon es muy complicado. Otra parte es increíble con nosotros." Ellie is happy now, but her heart is very complicated. Otherwise, she's incredible with us. Judy's Spanish is choppy and lacking in grammar, but she gets the point across. "No somos ricos, pero tenemos bastante . . . Entonces ella tiene educación." We are not rich, but we have plenty . . . As a result, she gets an education.

The heads of the Guatemalans bob up and down, mechanically.

"Ella toca violin." She plays the violin, as Judy holds her hands out to her left as if she were playing a violin. "Es increíble atleta." She's an incredible athlete. "Y despues cuatro meses ella habla todo ingles." After four months she speaks only in English. "Canta usted?" Judy asks Antonia. Do you sing? Because she sings very well.

As if violins and English weren't foreign enough to a poor family in Tiquisate, Judy produces photos of Ellie playing in the snow in northern Michigan. Antonia's eyes light up, and she exhales a quick breath. She is mesmerized by what she sees in front of her.

"Weee, frio." Cold. "Ella es bien bonita, gringa." She's a pretty white girl.

Maynor leans in, studies the white landscape on the photos on the table, and speaks for the first time. "Will Bereníce come and visit us?"

This is a good sign, and Judy knows it. She answers that Ellie will come, but that she's in school studying, and now is not a good time.

"She's beginning her school year this month in *los Estados Unidos*," Judy explains. "She loves studying art and music."

The Guatemalans nod their heads again, in unison. Technically, we speak the same language, they and I, but in reality, we don't understand each other at all. Violins, sports, snow, classical music—they've never been exposed to this stuff. Judy might as well be giving a lecture on Siberian linguistics.

"Bereníce and her father, Bob, are very *unidos*." Judy refers to Ellie as Bereníce for the first time, as she crosses her index and middle fingers.

"I have two other daughters who are twins: sixteen years old. *Tres chicas locas*." Judy shakes her head to emphasize a mother in distress. Three crazy girls. But Antonia just stares at Judy with a blank expression, as if to joke, "Try having ten."

"What grade is Bereníce in?" she asks instead.

"Sixth grade." Antonia's eyes widen again, and her mouth falls agape, as if one of her children had just completed a postdoctorate at an Ivy League school. "She began a little late because she had to learn English from scratch when she came to us," Judy continues.

"¿Esta muy alta?" Is she tall? Antonia returns to a subject that she can comprehend—physical appearance—while gazing at a picture of Ellie playing on the beach at the Frankfort Pier on Lake Michigan.

"No, she's not very tall. No one in my family is very tall."

Since this encounter began I have noticed Judy studying Antonia's physical appearance. Not quite like a doctor examining a patient, but more like a shopper sizing up avocados at the market. Judy is clearly worried about Antonia's health, and now her eyebrows rise, her face grows serious, and she asks the question point-blank.

"*Gracias a Dios*, I haven't been sick," the mother who has given birth to ten kids answers. "*Sólo Dios sábe porque* one doesn't get sick." Only God knows why.

"How old are you, Antonia?"

Forty years old. She lives with another man now, Antonia explains. But she suffers with him, too. He doesn't work because he's disabled. So the state pays him 600 quetzales [about $80] a month. "What can you do with 600 Q *a month*?"

"I try to work sometimes, too," Antonia continues. "But he won't let me work because he gets very jealous."

"What kind of work do you do?"

"I work making tortillas, but I only make 20 quetzales a day [$2.50] doing that."

Judy lets out a little giggle, sits back in her chair, and begins clapping her hands together as if she were hardening tortilla dough. "Sometimes when I try to make tortillas in the kitchen Ellie will stop me and say, 'No, no, cómo aquí.'" Like this. "Ella recuerda." She remembers how.

In this game of ping-pong between birth mother and adoptive mother, Antonia takes her turn, and the tone of the conversation swings back to desperation. It's clear that the Guatemalan woman doesn't think of making tortillas as a fun exotic occupation.

"I have suffered with my kids. Their father was always drunk, and he never helped me raise them. He hasn't been a father to them."

"Does he know we are here now?"

"Oh, no, he would be angry. Very angry."

"Does he know anything about Ellie? That she was adopted?"

"No, he knows nothing."

"Who does know what actually happened to her?"

"Just we here. Most of the family thinks that I have her in El Salvador."

Judy leans forward in her chair again and asks if it was difficult for Antonia to give Ellie up.

"Ay no." Antonia succumbs to exasperation and begins to sob. "Me sufrí mucho." I still remember my girl. Maynor follows suit, and his head goes back on the table.

"It was a very intelligent move," Judy's voice turns soft, "because her life is better now."

"I have suffered my whole life for giving her up."

"She is free now, *libre*."

Inching closer to Antonia, Judy tells her how Ellie remembers times when the family went to bed hungry, and she has told her daughter that was why Antonia had to do what she did.

"Sí," answers Antonia, slowly nodding her head.

"But Ellie also knows that you love her."

"I didn't want to give her up, but Cassandra, the owner, said that *la niña* should be taken because she was crying."

Not sadness but a look of defiance crosses Antonia's face now, and we can almost see the struggle between the temptation to relinquish her and the motherly instinct to keep her playing itself out in this tormented woman's bent eyebrows, her crinkled forehead.

"How did you originally get the idea to go to Cassandra?"

"A woman I know here who sells tortillas took me to Doña Cesy. It's her job. Doña Cesy takes babies. She lives in Pajacita, a town by Tecún Amán."

Tecún Amán is the legendary Mayan warrior who fought the Spanish conquistadores to the death, and legend has it that when he fell, the quetzal bird flew from an open wound in his chest to remain forever free in the Guatemalan highlands. But today Tecún Amán is a dirty and dangerous town on the Mexican border and a popular port of departure for *coyote* human traffickers and Colombian cocaine, all going north to the United States.

Antonia tells us there was a woman in Tiquisate who pressured her to give up her daughter. "There are plenty of women giving up kids for adoption."

"Do you know any of them?"

"I know lots of women here. One of them just went to Guate to have her child there. They suffer, these women. They work in brothels . . ." A pause follows. "But they say that adoption will be stopped . . ."

There's a chance, I tell her. Some don't like it, but there are lawyers and others fighting to give the kids a better life.

"So it won't shut down?" Antonia hangs on my every word.

"It's not a sure thing. It has shut down in other countries in Latin America where the governments feel like they are losing their kids."

Judy tries again to focus the conversation on Ellie. She tells me in English how she thinks her daughter's future is with Maynor more than poor Antonia. We ask what he remembers about his sister.

"I remember that I used to treat her rough. I used to hit her," he says in a subdued voice, his hands clasped together as if in prayer.

"But that's what siblings do," Judy confides to me in English. "It's okay." The eternal mother pauses a second, and then, "She throws the ball incredibly well. That's how we knew that she had brothers."

"She plays sports like a boy. She can throw a ball hundreds of meters, thanks to you, Maynor," I dramatize in Spanish.

Antonia and Maynor both smile. "A *varonila*. She's a *varonila*." A tomboy.

And suddenly the mood is joyous again. Just like that, by alluding to a recreation that anyone worldwide can understand. Where violins, choir, and snow only draw confused stares, sports draw laughter.

We ask Antonia how she felt today when she learned that we were here.

"Me sentí feliz." I was happy. "Miedo, no." I wasn't afraid. "Yo, contenta."

Antonia smiles wide now, drawing a quip from Judy about Ellie's pretty white teeth. "Gracias a Dios, digo yo, que encontró a alguien que . . ." Thank God, I say, that she met someone who . . . , and her voice trails off as she begins to weep again. Maynor does the same, and Judy pulls the photos closer to keep the dialogue flowing.

"Bien bonita." Very pretty, Antonia says as she dabs her eyes with a napkin and takes the last sip of her Coca-Cola.

"Lloró ella?" Did she cry? This is the first question that Antonia has asked about Ellie after she was abandoned.

"In the first three months after we adopted her she cried often when she was sad. "We thought she was in bed sleeping, but she was actually crying." Antonia and Maynor both break down again. And for the first time, Judy joins them. The calm in her voice that she's maintained throughout this crazy day erodes into shrieks and sobs. "Bob and I would hold her and tell her that everything was all right."

"Because of you guys she has a lovely and strong heart . . . I ahorita es gringita." Now she's a little white girl. Judy sniffles and dries her eyes. "But her heart is broken from losing you."

"Sí." Antonia nods, the resistant tone from earlier returning to her voice, followed by a pause. "You didn't bring her with you?"

"It wouldn't be right for this trip." Judy realizes that things may be going too well here. "We wanted to arrive here and meet you first. There are other Guatemalans who wouldn't want to reunite with their kids, and we were afraid because we didn't know how you'd react. We didn't want to hurt you."

"I never thought I'd hear from her again." Antonia sits back in her chair and assumes an air of confidence. "Some people speak badly about adoption. They say the kids are used for other purposes. But it's not like that. They say many things, like kids are used for their hearts, body parts. But I know it's for couples that can't have their own babies."

"Es verdad," Judy concurs.

"I thought Berenice was as good as lost," Antonia repeats. "I went to Antigua later on to ask about her. I wanted to find out if the señora could give me a telephone number. I went several times after they took the niña."

Judy asks if any money was exchanged. And suddenly, as if Judy's question were a lasso, Antonia's upper body shoots forward in the chair and her voice becomes animated again.

"A mi no. They gave money to Doña Cesy so that she'd bring me to Antigua."

"Was it her idea to take Ellie?" Judy is equal parts mother and detective.

"Pues, sí, but they didn't give me anything."

"How much money did Cesy make?"

"I don't know. She didn't tell me . . . Another woman told me that she received seven thousand quetzales [almost a thousand dollars]."

That amount is consistent with rumors I have been hearing from within the adoption community, I tell Judy.

"I don't know where Cesy is. They didn't give me anything." Antonia is almost livid now.

"What did Cesy tell you before you gave her up?"

"That if I gave her up, she'd be better off. She'd have great opportunities. A better life, with better parents."

"A better life, maybe, but better parents, no." Judy doesn't miss a beat.

"Esta bien," Antonia responds as she leans back in her chair again, appreciative of the compliment and somewhat subdued again.

"Ella era muy cariñosa conmigo." She was very loving with me, Antonia says as she raises her hands off the table and a look of concern spreads across her face. "She always wanted to be with me. *Todo, todo.* But when I became pregnant with another one I grew tired of handling her all the time, and I beat her often. *Yo le empujaba.*"

"Why?"

"Because she was very loving, my *niña.*" Antonia is sobbing uncontrollably, and her words fly out of her mouth along with drops of saliva. "But I had another in my belly, and I didn't want her. I beat her, *Usted,* and afterward I regretted it, but it was already too late." Antonia's voice quiets, and she mumbles to herself, almost in a whisper. "I hit my daughter because she loved me. She wrapped her arms around my stomach, but I had another inside.

"I didn't eat, I didn't drink, I just cried. She was so loving with me, and I treated her badly."

"And why did she do that?" Judy rationalizes this to me in English. "Because of her poverty and frustration. I know that Ellie has burn marks. She was burned with a stick."

"I don't know, *Usted.* I was just tired of handling her, because I had another."

Judy has regained her composure, and she sympathizes with Antonia in a way that only a mother could. "You know what, sometimes I do too . . . with my *hijas.*"

"You know, you lose it," she says in English. "I yell sometimes. I get mad, or impatient. It's normal in motherhood."

"But I beat her, *Usted*. She said, 'Mama, don't treat me like that. I love you a lot.' But I didn't. It was because of the pregnancy."

Judy leans back in her chair and nods her head, a combination of pity and understanding overtaking her. "She was trying to cope."

Just then the phone at the front desk rings, removing us suddenly from this elevated moment of truth and clarity and dropping us back into the daily world of chaos and struggle. We've found Antonia and reentered Ellie's past, Antonia has embraced us and the opportunity to reunite with the daughter she gave up, and it appears we've done all this without putting anyone in danger. But what happens now? Do we end this moment in a respectful manner, get ourselves back to Antigua, and reestablish the border between rich and poor, American and Guatemalan? And is it fair to make the family wait for months, even years, before they are allowed to meet Ellie again?

"When Bereníce is a little older would be a good time to bring her down here. *Cuando ella tiene dieciseis, diecisiete, diechiocho años, es buen tiempo.*" Judy emphasizes patience. When she is sixteen, seventeen, or eighteen would be a good time. "*Ahora no es buen tiempo.*"

But the adoptive mother is unwilling to leave it at that. Instead, Judy suggests that we invite Maynor to return to Antigua with us—to foster this new relationship with Ellie's brother, who, she says, represents the future. Judy lends Maynor and Junior her camera and suggests that they walk around Tiquisate to take more photos for us—of the house where they lived, of the market: places where we shouldn't go.

"In the meantime," she says, "I'd also like to talk to her about the prostitution and the burns."

But at the suggestion of joining us for a few days in Antigua, Maynor insists on bringing his mother along, too. There's no question that he's loyal.

"So you can leave whenever you want? There's no risk if you don't return to your house today?"

"No, there's no danger," Antonia answers, her face growing stern again, suggesting an air of confidence that seems to come and go like a flickering light switch. It seems evident why Cassandra diagnosed her with psychosomatic symptoms when Antonia relinquished Ellie, and why the adoption lawyer was easily able to turn away the grieving birth mother after Antonia changed her mind and returned to Antigua to see the girl.

"It's that I want to go with my son. My boyfriend never provides for me, and it's up to me to find food to eat. He doesn't give me anything. So sometimes I tell him that I need to go work. He can't tell me what to do."

Does Antonia think this strange white woman who appeared out of nowhere today is trying to run away with another one of her kids, or does she just want to come along for the ride?

Maynor raises his head from the table and settles the score: "I'd like to go with my mom."

Understanding that this is a united family despite the poverty, despite the abuse, despite the lost daughter, Judy accedes to the wish of Ellie's oldest brother and accepts the idea of bringing them both along.

Though she doesn't completely realize it yet, Judy is slowly adopting the whole family. Not just a window to Ellie's past is opening up, but a whole wall is being taken down, brick by brick.

9 ❧ Sad Truth

There's a wonderful scene in John Sayles's fictional movie *Casa de los babys* where an Irish American woman from Boston who is living in a hotel in a Central American country while she waits to adopt her baby engages in a touching conversation with a local maid who comes to clean her sheets and fluff her pillows. The adoptive mother doesn't speak a lick of Spanish, yet she tells the maid in English how she dreams of days when the schools in Boston are closed due to snow so she can take her child ice skating out on Jamaica Pond. The maid, who doesn't speak any English, pauses and sits on the bed while listening attentively, and then shares her own story, in Spanish, of how she couldn't care for her first child, and gave it up for adoption. She then tells the adoptive mother how she hopes the child ended up with someone like her. Both women realize they've reached some deep connection in their conversation, even though neither one understands what the other said.

In the bedroom at Hotel Familiar I find Judy and Antonia, lying on their sides on twin single beds, facing each other, the fan turned on full blast, and the television, though muted, showing a Spanish soap opera called *Tres Mujeres*, apparently about three women constantly meeting each other in a living room and engaging in heated arguments. I take a seat on the edge of one bed, near Antonia's feet, and Judy tells me how much she's learned from this strange woman in just fifteen minutes alone with her in the room.

"She told me she's given up five of her ten kids for adoption!" Judy blurts out, almost laughing. "Ellie is the last of the five. She says she's been paid for all the others."

My jaw drops. This is the information I have been dying to ask about. It's also the reason so many Guatemalans cite for wanting to shut down international adoption—what they call "an industry," though organizations like UNICEF have been hard-pressed to document a single case of a woman being paid to give up her baby.

"You were *paid* to give up your children?" I turn to Antonia and ask. And the ease with which the birth mother opens up to me and answers my questions, as if I were a trustworthy grandfather, or a priest, surprises the heck out of us.

Yes, and she fully expected to receive money for Ellie, too. Antonia says that Cassandra, the Hogar Nuevo Día lawyer, told her, or at least implied, that she would get approximately 5,000 quetzales (about $625) once she relinquished her seven-year-old girl. But it never happened, and after they took teary-eyed Ellie away, telling Antonia that she was an unfit mother and that the girl would enjoy a better life in the hands of Americans, she left for El Salvador in a fit of guilt and depression.

Antonia tells me she received between 4,000 and 7,000 quetzales (between $500 and $875) for each of the first four, though the adoptions were facilitated through lawyers other than Cassandra and Clayton. Neither Ellie, Maynor, nor William knew the first three, Cindy Siomara, Cindy Estefania, and Alicia, because they were given up as infants. But the one named Erik? No, he didn't die, even though he was a malnourished, sickly looking boy. He was given up for adoption at age four, and, Antonia thinks, ended up with a family in France, or at least that's what her lawyer told her years later. She tells me a photo arrived one day, several years later, of Erik, happy and healthy, in a snowsuit and wearing skis, with mountains in the background. The French Alps? we wonder.

And the others? Antonia remembers only that one of the girls ended up with a family in Tierra Santa. It would take months before I realized what she meant by that. Tierra Santa translated means "Holy Land" . . . Jerusalem! Yes, this dirt-poor woman from the southern coast of Guatemala apparently has children in the United States, France, and . . . Israel.

"That's how I built the house where we lived with Esvin," Antonia states in a firm tone. "With my own money."

"With what money?" I ask incredulously. "From selling tortillas?"

"No, from the others I gave up," Antonia responds, apparently oblivious to the horrified expressions that Judy and I exchange. She built a house for her family with the money the lawyers paid her to give up her children, and then Esvin brought home Esperanza and booted them onto the street, and because she was so poor, she later gave up Erik and Ellie too, though the benefits she expected from giving up her last daughter never arrived . . . until now.

This is not what an adoptive parent wants to learn about the biological mother of her child: that she has sunk into a pattern of selling babies over and over again.

"If they paid you thousands of quetzales for every other kid before Beren*í*ce, why didn't they pay you for her too?"

"¿Saber?" Who knows? "But maybe because another woman took me there: I don't how much they gave her. I was just waiting and waiting for them to give me money. And they never gave me anything. They never gave me a single cent."

"Was that part of it, that she really needed the money?" Judy asks me in English, expressing her amazement at Antonia's level of openness.

"No, what happened was that I gave her up because the *muchacha* went there with me and told me, 'Give her up, *porque esa niña va bien . . . de la.*'" Because the girl will be well off . . . give her up. "But because she was older I didn't want to give her up. And *la niña* said, 'Mama, I want to go, I want to go.'"

"Beren*í*ce said she wanted to go?" I ask.

"*Sí*, she said, 'I want to go with that woman named Cesy, to *la capital*.' That girl showed up and convinced Ellie to come along."

"Did she give Ellie a gift?"

"¿Saber, Usted?" Who knows, sir?

"And so my girl said, 'I want to go. If you don't want to go, then I'll go alone.' Cesy told me that she'd take her to Doña Cassandra.

She gives kids up for adoption. 'No,' I told her. 'I don't want to give her up because the girl is already older. There's a mistake.' 'No,' Cesy told me. 'Don't worry . . . the kids will have a good life. *Los niños van bien* . . . And they'll give you money,' she told me.

"'Ay no,' I told her. '*Me da lástima*. It hurt me. No,' I told her. 'Eeeehh,' I protested. But I went to Antigua with her. We stayed for one night in a *pensión*, and the next day we went to give her up."

"Did Beren*í*ce know what was happening?"

"I told her lies. I told her, '*Mi hija*, you will stay here. Tomorrow I'll arrive to get you.'"

Judy has leaned over the side of the bed toward Antonia, following every word, every blink of the woman's eyes.

"'*Mañana*, I'll come to get you.' But I was lying to her. And they told me later that she was asking, 'When is my mom going to come get me? *¿Cúando? ¿Cúando?* And she was crying."

An argument has been resolved on the television screen, and the two women in the room are hugging each other, though we can tell from the predictable plotline of the soap opera that they will soon find something else to fight about.

Judy feels comfortable enough to ask Antonia about almost anything, and so she goes for the next big one. "I think it's safe now for us to ask her about prostitution," she tells me in English as she props up her head with her right elbow.

"Beren*í*ce remembers that times were hard because you were very poor . . ." I tiptoe with my words and try to deal the blow as softly as possible. These are invasive questions, and I feel uncomfortable asking them. "And that sometimes you had to do different jobs to bring home money . . . She says you had sex for money . . . It's okay, Beren*í*ce understands why you did that. Because without food you couldn't have survived."

"Ah, sí pues." Antonia's face reddens, and she brings her hand up to cover her mouth, like a little girl. She admits to being a sex worker, "but only five or six times, no more," and only after Esvin left her for another woman and kicked them out of the house.

"Did Bereníce or the other kids ever watch you have sex?" Judy asks.

"No," Antonia responds emphatically. "She never knew. But the neighbor told everyone. That's how they found out."

"Where did it happen?"

"Al otra lado." It always happened "on the other side," or in the other room of the gray wooden house by the *jocote* tree where Ellie remembers living after Esvin abandoned them.

Judy and I hold our tongues and just nod. Today isn't a day for judgment. It's just about making contact and gathering information.

"How did the men treat Bereníce? Was there contact between her and the men sometimes?"

"Ay, no! I lived with an old man for a while, but other than that, no. He treated me badly. She didn't like him, so I threw him out. I was afraid he'd hurt her, but he never did."

Antonia's defiance then disappears and gives way to humility. "She said this all about me?" Antonia asks, her voice quiets to a whisper and a twinge of guilt comes over her.

"Bereníce."

"She told you this?"

"Yes, she remembers."

"Then she must have seen me do it."

"Pues," I say. "But she loved you too, because you were her mother, and you gave her love, even though the work was hard."

"I had three kids in school during this time, but times were difficult and they weren't able to study." Antonia's voice cracks. She is clearly trying to defend herself. "Maynor, William, and Bereníce were all in school. They reached the second grade, *más o menos*."

Judy also understands that we're putting Antonia on the spot, and she doesn't feel comfortable doing so. Cutting her down to size is not a good idea, especially when we want Antonia to feel positive about herself and excited to meet Ellie again, someday. Judy switches gears in an attempt to guide the conversation out of the darkness and into the light.

"Let's ask about church," she tells me in English. "We may even find out about the mysterious candle ceremony." The adoptive mother clearly enjoys this detective work.

"Are you religious?"

"*Yo*, no. But Maynor, *sí*. He's an Evangelist."

"How is it that he's an Evangelist but you're not?"

"He needed to enter the church because his girlfriend is a member. She said if he didn't join, she wouldn't marry him."

"Are they together, those two?"

"She'll turn fifteen this December, and her father doesn't like him, so they aren't together right now. She's very in love with him, and he's in love with her too. But her father hit him and broke his nose."

"Ellie remembers a story from after Esvin left you, that you performed a ceremony, maybe religious, in the house with candles and urine. You told all the kids to go in the house, you closed the windows, lit the candles, and asked the kids to urinate in a bowl, and then you drank it."

"I don't remember that. ¿Saber, Usted?" Who knows? "*Yo no me recuerdo.*"

"Bereníce told us this happened shortly after her father left."

"*¿Saber?*" Who knows? "*Sí*, we had candles, because a neighbor who was a witch would arrive at my house sometimes to perform ceremonies with bottles full of candles. *Veladoras.* The neighbor came in my house and said it was cursed. People in town called her a witch."

"But was there urine?"

"I don't remember that. *La niña* might remember, but I don't."

Or maybe Antonia had willed herself to forget some of these sad memories. Just as Cesy had urged her with respect to relinquishing Ellie: try to forget, or deny this stuff ever happened.

❧

At 2:15 in the afternoon, less than two hours after meeting Antonia and Maynor, Judy and I pile with them into the pickup truck owned by the proprietor of the Hotel Familiar. They had originally lobbied for Maynor and Ellie's brother William to join us as well, but he is in the hospital with an infection and the staff won't let him leave, so off we go, the four of us, leaving Tiquisate for Escuintla, where Judy and I began our day. Antonia sits in the cab to the right of the driver, and Judy, Maynor, and I crawl into the bed of the truck, half sitting and half lying down, with our backs up against the rear window of the cab.

Maynor seems more comfortable with us now and talks freely, pointing out the pineapple groves and sugarcane fields spreading out behind us as we head north for the Pacific highway. We can hardly hear him as the whistle of the wind and the groan of the pickup's motor drown out his voice, but on his face Maynor reveals his pride in this region he calls home.

"*Mire*, look at all that fruit," he is yelling now. "And that strong smell. That's rotten fruit that has been left out in the sun."

But Maynor is still wearing only the black Diesel T-shirt he had on when they arrived at the hotel. To avoid raising suspicion, he and Antonia did not go home to get more clothes, if they even have more, that is. So when we turn right onto the Pacific highway and speed up to what must be sixty miles per hour, the boy begins to shake. These people are from the blisteringly hot Costa Sur, and any change in temperature or strong wind will give them the chills.

Maynor is sitting on his knees in the middle of the pickup's bed, pointing out the beautiful landscape to us like a tour guide when Judy invites him to join us directly behind the cab's window, which shields us from the wind. He crawls over to her left, pulls his knees up under his chin, and, to our amazement, places his head on her shoulder. Judy wraps her left arm around Maynor and pulls him tight and looks over at me.

"This kid is hardwired for love," she tells me, as tropical Guatemala flies by all around us. "He is not afraid of being affectionate . . . just like Ellie was when she came to us."

We arrive at the Motel Texas around 4:00 p.m., exhausted and hungry from the day's events, just as an afternoon September rain begins to fall. Judy books three rooms for us, and this time we'll stay the night. She occupies number 20, I take number 16, and Antonia and Maynor share number 8. After dropping off our belongings we head back to the poolside tables for a well-deserved meal (amid all the drama we had forgotten to eat lunch), and find that after only two minutes of being in their room, the Guatemalans have padlocked their door from the inside. Are they taking advantage of the novelty of a good lock or being overly paranoid?

We sit under a tent canopy and read the menus while watching the raindrops interact with the pool's azure-blue surface. Antonia expresses amazement at the exorbitant prices of the food (everything costs between 40–60 quetzales, $5–7.50), and Maynor follows suit, trying to order the cheapest thing on the menu. But Judy will have none of it and orders him a juicy steak and a bottle of Coke. Meat is a profound luxury to the poor. To celebrate the successful reunion, she and I order Cuba libres, but they have so little rum in them that we buy another bottle of rum and several more Cokes.

"When Ellie was younger she was frustrated because she couldn't speak English yet, but I told Bereníce just to be patient," Judy recalls. "'By Christmastime you'll get it,' I told her. And it was true: it took her only four months." Judy seems to be jumping back and forth between Guatemala and northern Michigan in her comments, referring to "Bereníce" one moment and "Ellie" the next. "*Pero tiene un poquito* aaaa-ccent." But she has a slight accent. Judy draws out the vowels and says the *a* in a nasal, midwestern pronunciation.

I look over at Maynor, who is struggling to cut the steak in front of him as he grips the knife as he would a baton, halfway up the shaft and in the wrong hand. Judy reaches over the table and corrects him, and the boy smiles, as if delighted to learn a new skill.

"Are you an Evangelist because of your girlfriend or because of God?" I ask him.

"Por Dios," he answers in a proud tone, his chin rising an inch. For God.

"We're in trouble here." Judy looks at me and rolls her eyes.

North American Evangelical missionaries have been invading Central American in droves in recent years, teaching the natives to reject the Catholic Church and to refrain from drinking and smoking or singing and dancing outside of church lest they offend their God.

I return Judy's concern with a chuckle. "At least his religion is keeping him away from gangs or violence or drugs," I say.

"You like to sing?" Judy asks him. She's already drawing parallels between Maynor and Ellie. "What kinds of songs?"

"Anything from *la Biblia*," he beams.

Like a couple of detectives, our conversation returns briefly to the relinquishment of Ellie. We ask Antonia some of the same questions from earlier in the day, to see if the answers change, or if she remembers or reveals any more information.

"Did it happen because of the woman who was encouraging it, or did you also think it was a good idea?"

Antonia says she resisted at first, but the *jaladora* Cesy showed up again eight days later. It's for the gringos who can't have babies of their own, she was told.

"I said I couldn't do it. 'Bien,' she said. 'They'll pay you for her.' 'Ay, no,' I said, but they convinced me."

Cesy and Estela accompanied Antonia and the boys from Tiquisate to Guatemala City and then Antigua, leaving early in the morning to avoid attracting attention. Cesy certainly knew that baby trafficking is a dangerous taboo in rural Guatemala, and that's why she told Antonia to keep this a secret. But what about Estela, the woman from Tiquisate? What was her role in this?

"No, she followed us. She just finds the women . . ."

"There it is," Judy concludes in English. "They are out there working the field."

Once they arrived at the office in Antigua, Antonia recalls a *cuidadora*, or foster mother who looks after the relinquished children, arriving to take her away. "I began to cry, but Berenice told me, 'Mama, stop crying.'"

"How did you know these women?" Judy asks.

"They knew about me and just showed up at the house, because that's their work."

"But why then? Why not earlier? Bereníce was already seven years old."

No answer.

"And why the girl and not the boys?" Judy asks me in English, nodding toward Maynor sitting there, his athletic hands busy practicing the new steak-cutting method.

"When you made the decision to give up a child for adoption . . . ," the question is slow and deliberate, "why the girl and not the boys?"

"*No sé.* That's what they told me to do. They didn't want the others." She nods toward Maynor. "They wanted her." Antonia is confused. She doesn't understand why we would want to know this.

The answer, though, is blatantly obvious when considering the demographics of international adoption. Girls are much more sought after than boys are, especially in China, where the vast majority of abandoned children are female. According to the adoptive parents I'd spoken to, the motherly instinct drives women more than men to push for adopting a child. And when it came to those families, the woman's first choice was usually for a daughter.

"And when did you see her last?"

"When they took her away, to the girl who arrived in a car."

"And Maynor and William were nearby?"

"They saw her in the window, driving away."

Judy and I agree in English that it must have been Cassandra, the lawyer, who wanted the girl. Whether Antonia was prepared, or could have been convinced, to give up her boys: who knows? Ellie remembers leaving the office first, walking hand-in-hand with another woman, not aware yet what was happening. They put her in the car, and that's when she saw her brothers through the rearview window, running after the car and waving to her.

When she was adopting Ellie, Judy says, Cassandra told her that the appearance of the brothers was an unwelcome surprise. They were hanging around outside the office and peeking in the windows like little animals, according to Cassandra, who also said she'd never admit rowdy boys like that into Hogar Nuevo Día.

"Was this the same *animal* she was referring to?" Judy fixes her eyes on Maynor, who is smiling and adeptly cutting his steak by now. "I am just floored by his appearance compared to what Cassandra told me."

Antonia has been shoveling rolled-up tortillas stuffed with rice into her mouth. She ceases for a moment and looks toward me for her turn to ask a question. "I want to know something. How much are they getting for a child, because the people here don't give hardly anything to a poor woman?"

I tell her that I hear some lawyers in the capital are making as much as $12,000 per child.

Antonia's eyes widen. She can't imagine an amount of money this large. "And I hear these days that some women are receiving 20,000 quetzales [$2,750] to transport a child," she answers. "When I gave up the *niña*, they told me they'd give me 7,000, and they gave me nothing."

"Are some people having babies just to sell them?" Judy asks.

Without pause Antonia nods her head. "Hay muchas." There are plenty. In El Salvador, women abandon their kids for that purpose, she adds.

"How much do *you* have to pay for adoption?" She looks straight at Judy.

I tell her that an American family pays between $20,000 and $30,000 for an adoption.

Antonia's gaze returns to me, studying my face as if she's about to cross-examine me. She asks whether I think it's possible for a woman here to make a living selling her babies. The no-nonsense tone in her voice creeps me out, because I wonder if she's actually considering having more babies just for money.

Instead of answering, I throw the question back at her. "What do you think of this, *adopción* . . . people paying women for their babies?"

"No," Antonia replies, flustered, as if breaking down and changing her testimony under oath. "What happened is that they told me they were helping the kids, that I couldn't take care of them." She begins to weep, and then, through sobs, "But they took my *niña* without paying."

A long silence follows, weighed down by the tension in the air. I finish my Cuba libre and pour myself another one, a stiff one.

This talk of selling babies is so foreign and scary to Judy that she needs to reconnect with something familiar. She borrows my cellular phone, walks to the other end of the pool, and calls Bob back in Traverse City. "We found her." We can overhear Judy's excited words over the placid water. "She and Ellie's brother are here with us in a hotel, eating dinner . . . I know, I can't believe it either . . . ," she says before she walks to her room to talk in private.

"What about Esvin, their father?" I ask Antonia once Judy returns from the phone call.

"Nada. He was always drinking the day away. He was never around, and he claimed the kids weren't his."

"What did he drink?"

"Liquor," Maynor answers, nodding his head when I ask about the *aguardiente* that has turned many a peasant farmer into a sad drunk.

"Ellie remembers that things were going to be okay, but then he left with another woman."

"Esperanza," Antonia says in a spiteful tone. "She encouraged Esvin to be nasty and hit the kids."

"Is she still with him?"

"*Sí*, and they still live in my house."

"But what does she see in him if he's drunk all the time?"

"Por el amor de la casita." She wants the house."

"Does Esperanza drink too?" I ask.

"She used to . . . She's an *Evangélica* now."

By the look on Judy's face, she has another list of questions on her mind to ask, probably from Bob. She instructs me to ask Antonia about family planning and whether she intends to have more children.

"Do you use condoms? Are their condoms in Tiquisate?"

Antonia nods her head while chewing her steak. "Sí hay, en el Centro de Salud." In the health center. "But who knows if they give them to women like me? I never use them."

"And Esvin?"

"¿Saber?" Who knows? "He never liked them."

"But there are also medicine pills that prevent future pregnancies," I tell Antonia. Does she even know about birth control pills? I wonder.

"When I was pregnant with Cindy Siomara I was planning to stop having any more kids, but the medicine didn't work for me. One day I would take it, the next I wouldn't."

"Is it possible that you could have more babies?" Judy asks her point-blank.

"Saber? I think I could still have them, because when I was younger the midwife told me I would have eighteen. And I trust her."

"Oh, Lord, here we go." Judy falls back in her chair.

"Do you want more babies?"

"Pues, right now I don't know. But when my boys are older I might like to have more, because they will leave me, and I'll be alone in the house."

"Others to help you in the house or to give up for adoption?"

"No, para la casa." Antonia looks annoyed.

Trying not to judge, Judy nevertheless offers Antonia advice. "In the States, when you are more than forty years old, it's better to become a *grandmother*, and no more *mother*."

I explain. Antonia should wait for Maynor to have kids. She doesn't need any more herself.

"So I can't have any more?" she asks, disappointed.

Waist deep in a potentially ugly cultural clash now, I try to back out slowly. "You've already had ten kids and given five of them up," I tell Antonia. "And you hardly have enough food or money for the two you still do have under your care. Maybe it's time . . . We're preaching . . . ." I stop and turn to Judy.

"And that's okay," she assures me. "As long as we tell her, 'This is how we do things,' without telling her, 'This is how you *should* do things.'"

"Eso es lo que hacen los gringos." That's what the white people do. "In our culture we don't need to have eighteen kids: just a few, like two or three or four. But it's just a cultural difference."

"*Pues*, my grandmother had twenty," Antonia counters.

"And how much pain and suffering and hunger was there?" Judy asks in English.

"Did your grandmother have food for all?"

"They planted beans and rice and corn, and yucca, tomatoes, and peppers. When the kids got older they helped their father cultivate the land."

"And are they still alive?"

"No, some have died. Diabetics, others from drinking."

"Did any of them die when they were younger?"

"I think about four of them died just after they were born."

"There was enough food for everyone?"

"Yes, at the time there was."

"But in the States we need food, but also education . . . and enough money so that we don't suffer. That's why we have fewer children."

I translate: "The idea for many Americans is that if they have fewer kids, those kids will have more money and opportunities. That's to say, if you have four kids instead of twenty, those four could go to school and study. There are more opportunities for them. It's just a different idea."

"And here there are families who have a bunch of *niños* and don't send them to school." Antonia echoes what we are saying. "There is no money."

"But if your grandmother had had three or four instead of twenty, she could have used the money that she spent on raising twenty to send the three or four to school," Judy continues.

"Mira pues." Look here. Antonia knows she has been pushed into a corner, and she doesn't like it. Her voice raises an octave. "I've gone eight years without having a kid. I can't have kids because I'm sick, *de mi matriz* [in my uterus]. The last one was Alicia, who I gave up for adoption. I have pain in the ovaries, so bad that sometimes I can't eat."

"Another reason not to have any more babies," responds Judy, and then says in English, "She doesn't look good down there. She's sick."

"The uterus is a muscle, and hers has clearly been overworked. Antonia, is there a doctor in Tiquisate who can help you?"

"Sí, una comadrona." A midwife. "Her name is Naya, but she already died, about four years ago."

"Do you know of anyone else?"

"There's another woman at a clinic, but she charges a lot: five hundred quetzales [sixty-five dollars] to cure my uterus."

A pause.

"Or maybe I could visit the woman from the Evangelical church who can pray away the curses in my body. She only charges a hundred Q."

"Are you cursed?"

"¿Saber, Usted?" Who knows? "Witches have entered my uterus . . . and the only way to cure me is to pray them away. Only God knows what's wrong with me."

The tape recorder clicks off as the ribbon reaches its end. A sign of mercy? I wonder. What else can we possibly ask this woman now?

But instead of flipping over the tape and continuing the interview, the four of us finish our dinners and catch a cab to a shopping center in Escuintla to treat our Guatemalan friends to dessert. We order ice cream cones: Judy and I, some exotic multicolored flavors that we learned about growing up in the United States; Maynor and Antonia ask for just plain chocolate—the rich, dark color of extravagant wealth.

Antonia inhales her dessert in what seems like thirty seconds, and then she moves in on her son's territory. Maynor holds his cone in his right hand, imitating Judy and me, and between licks, his mother picks out pieces of creamy chocolate with her bare dirty thumb and forefinger and shovels them into her mouth as if they were wontons lathered in sweet-and-sour sauce.

10 ❧ The Storm

Excerpt from a letter Maynor writes to Ellie on September 30, 2005 (translated version):

Berenice,

These days that I've spent with your mom have been the happiest days of my life. I know that even though my mamá gave you up, we are not angry [with her], you know, because you know that we have nothing to eat, and that's why my mother did it, for me and for William, and she wronged us because we want to know and see you and be able to hug you and kiss you like we know your mamá, I have hope to know you and be able to see you and talk with you. I know that someday you'll return. My mamá cried a lot [when she met Judy] and we, me and William, cried when we remembered what we did before with you. We beat you and that's why we want to know you to ask for forgiveness because we feel sad when we remember how poorly we behaved with you.

I ask you to continue forward, don't stray from the path and don't look back. Continue forward, because we never were able to study, we regret, you know that, because of my papa we couldn't study, you know, mine and your father drinks a lot, he is lost in alcohol, he lost all hope.

I still remember when they took you in the car and you said "good-bye" to us with your hand [waving]. We cried a lot at that moment because you were never to return. We made a mistake and we still make mistakes. I wish you were with us and that we were together, you, William, me and my mamá, but I know that you don't want that because you already have everything with Lluri [Judy] and with my mamá you don't have what they have. I know that we will meet again and we will be able to talk with you.

Judy's final night together with Maynor in Antigua is a bittersweet one. She has spent a week with him here after sending Antonia back to Tiquisate after just one night to avoid stirring up any suspicions. I have been by their side in the paradise of the rich these seven days, dining at nice restaurants, visiting the market with them, serving as documentarian and occasional translator, and watching the sixteen-year-old boy change as he is exposed to the world outside his poor little village. Maynor is now adept at holding a knife and fork when he eats steak; he wants to begin studying again and is reading Spanish-language workbooks and writing in a journal that Judy bought for him; he talks of a desire forming inside of him to learn enough English so that he can come and visit Ellie in the United States.

All week Maynor has carried Judy's day pack on his shoulders and her Sony camera in his pocket. He has stopped to take pictures seemingly every other second, not realizing that film is expensive and that he has shot the same storefronts, the same churches, the same cobblestone streets, and the same white tourists over and over again, only because he has never seen them before and they fascinate him. One day I take Maynor to the local cinema to see *Star Wars Episode II: Attack of the Clones*, and catch him taking pictures inside the theater, not of Anakin Skywalker wielding his light saber but of people sitting in the audience eating popcorn. Naturally, the photo doesn't turn out, and Maynor laments that he won't be able to show it to his brother William.

With every passing second Judy feels more like a mother to this boy, she tells me. Does her statement reflect a sense of cultural entitlement? Perhaps, but it also reflects Judy's somewhat naive, yet genuine, bigheartedness. In Maynor she sees a sweet, caring, and generous young man. And she can't help but remember the week she spent in

Antigua with Ellie, before the adoption paperwork went through, five years before.

"I wanted to keep studying and stay in school," he tells us as he bursts into tears over his steak the last night we are together. "But when Esvin came home drunk and saw us sitting with books open in front of us, he would slam our heads down on the table. 'Books won't earn you any money,' he yelled." And so they dropped out of school—Maynor, William, Berenice, and Erik—and began working in the market.

"I don't want to adopt him," Judy assures me. "He's much too old for that, and I don't have the money. But if we can enroll him in a good school here in Antigua, we can still change his life and give him some of the same opportunities Ellie is getting." One of the places we have visited is Safe Passage, a nonprofit organization started by a woman from Maine that helps impoverished Guatemalan kids, most of whom virtually grew up in the capital city's sprawling garbage dump. Safe Passage's Antigua branch gives them a *hogar* to live in while they return to school, and if they attend classes diligently, they are given a bag of food to take back to their mothers every few months.

The problem is, Maynor is deeply involved in the Evangelical church back in Tiquisate, and he's also in love with his girlfriend, Guadalupe, who told Maynor she wouldn't marry him unless he converted and joined her at church. He's not ready to leave home yet, so Judy just asks him to think about Safe Passage, hoping the week of spoiling him in Antigua will help.

"There's no future for you if you don't get an education," Judy tells Maynor. "You'll end up working like an animal in the *finca* just like most people in your village . . . But if you join the program, I will sponsor you, and you can go to the bilingual school across the street from the *hogar* so that when Berenice visits, you can communicate with her . . . You know that if you learn English, in this country you can get whatever work you want, and someday you can buy a big house back in Tiquisate for your mom and your brother and your girlfriend . . . but it would mean leaving them for a while."

The offer leaves Maynor speechless, and we can tell from the glimmer in his eyes that he is considering this. Maybe, just maybe, for the first time in his life, he is beginning to dream.

ॐ

When Maynor and I wake up at the hotel Lazos Fuertes on the morning of Tuesday, October 4, Judy is already gone. She caught a 5:00 a.m. shuttle bus to the airport for her flight back to the United States, and the big questions now are whether Maynor will choose to leave his girlfriend and study in Antigua and how long Judy will wait before telling Ellie the whole truth about the discovery of her birth family. "She's a teenager, and that's hard enough on a girl," Judy told me the night before. "I'll talk this through with Bob, but I don't think we want to tell her until we're prepared to make the trip down for the reunion."

The rain is pouring down in torrents when Maynor and I leave the hotel and walk through the market and the bus terminal where we'll leave for Escuintla and then Tiquisate so I can deliver him home to Antonia. This is the rainy season, of course, but I've never seen sheets falling down this early in the day, and it rained all night, too. On the front page of the *Prensa Libre*, Guatemala's national newspaper, is a horrific scene of a mother and several children huddled together in a flat-bottomed boat, plastic parkas over their shoulders, and anxious looks on their faces as they float through what looks like a flooded village. The picture was taken in a town in the Costa Sur, not too far from Maynor's home, and the newspaper's headline reads, "Country in Red Alert; Rains Will Continue for 48 Hours." Hurricane Stan has hit the fragile Central American isthmus, following on the heels of Hurricane Katrina, which destroyed much of New Orleans a month ago, and Rita, which scared the daylights out of Houston. Thousands of Guatemalans are being evacuated, the *Prensa Libre* reports; tens of thousands more are at risk of losing their homes; and President Oscar Berger is appealing to the United States for help.

How much damage can rain do? I naively think. Guatemalans

have been through all kinds of hardship, and this is the time of year for water; they can certainly handle a few days of it. My thoughts are focused on getting Maynor back to Tiquisate without raising anyone's suspicions, and monitoring how he reacts to returning to his impoverished village. The first leg of our journey is easy, and the constant drumming of raindrops on the roof of the chicken bus lulls me to sleep. I have a Guatemalan companion on the seat next to me, so I don't have to worry about getting pickpocketed. But the bus from Escuintla to Tiquisate breaks down on the highway, halfway there, and Maynor and I stand outside in the rain so we can hail another ride. By the time we arrive in Tiquisate we are soaking wet and hungry. So I treat us to lunch at a pizza restaurant with a roof over it near the bus terminal, and watch with interest as Maynor looks up and down the main street of the only place he has ever known. Three-wheeled Tuc-tuc taxis come and go; men and women who look older than they actually are carry heavy sacks on their shoulders; others sit in doorways, utterly bored, fanning their faces with whatever objects they can find. The stifling midday heat makes the scene in front of us swim before my eyes. Do things look different to Maynor now? I wonder.

He leads me down a series of dirt paths, by a paved basketball court and a church called La Shalom, to the three-walled concrete shack where Antonia, her boyfriend, Wagner, Maynor, and William live; judging by the condition of their home, *survive* might be more apt. The corrugated tin sheet that serves as a roof over their kitchen and living space and keeps out most of the rain is held up by a couple of wobbly posts and a tree. The clothesline stretching from one post to the other does not protect the garments and old shirts with hollowed-out armpits from the water, and at least one pair of pants hanging from the clothesline reaches down to the muddy ground below. The blue *pila* for washing dishes, and probably second-rate showers too, is filled with stinky dark water.

And there, sitting on three plastic green chairs on the only dry spot of ground, are Antonia, her disabled boyfriend, Wagner, and William, Maynor's younger brother who has just returned from the hospital.

Antonia wears a flowery pink shirt that hangs down over her belly, a black skirt with pink and green water lilies on it, and blue flip-flops—functional and presentable clothing. I shoot photos of the scene around me with my digital camera to show Judy and, when the time comes, Ellie, too. Wagner, the jealous boyfriend who won't let Antonia work, seems docile enough. He wears a white sleeveless T-shirt, black jeans, and tennis shoes—almost identical to William's outfit, and I laugh to myself as I notice that the boyfriend looks almost as young as the boys do. Late twenties or early thirties, I think.

Antonia is sad today. She tells me the photos of Ellie that Judy had given her the week before when we met at the Hotel Familiar were left out in the rain in their manila envelope, and now they are barely visible. She apologizes and asks if Judy can send more.

I ask Antonia to guide me through the rest of their home so I can take photos and show Judy the condition in which they live. One-half of the concrete structure is a bedroom where the family sleeps: two on the firm mattress on the one-person-size bed and two on a blanket on the concrete floor. The walls of the room are decorated with pink and yellow plywood, and the only possessions in the room are a tiny black-and-white television sitting on a plastic stool, a cheap fan, a plastic clock hanging from a nail on the wall, a garbage basket, and a towel hanging over a corner window to keep the sun out in the early morning. The other room is an addition to the original concrete block with tin sheets forming its three walls, but this is not enough to keep out the rainwater, and when we enter the room we wade in a half inch of slop. Here the family stores a few busted plastic fans, buckets, shampoo, plastic cups, blankets, and the two or three sets of clothing each person owns, stacked neatly on a table against the filthy wall.

Behind the concrete structure is another addition someone made by nailing a few tin sheets together. Inside is a barely functional toilet with a cushioned white seat and a lid that hangs off to one edge as if playing dead. Next to the toilet bowl is a blue basin filled with muddy water for flushing. I decide against looking inside the toilet.

When I return to the open area under the corrugated roof, Maynor is beaming with pride as he shows his mother and brother the photos he took of Antigua. "Lluri [Judy, he means], Jacobo [me], and I ate here, we stayed at that hotel, and this is the *parque* where Lluri took Bereníce after she adopted her." Maynor shows William the Spanish workbook Judy bought for him to encourage him to return to school, and William holds the book delicately in his hands as if it were the Holy Grail.

"What language is this?" William asks me, and I remember that, according to Maynor, this fifteen year old didn't even make it through the first grade before dropping out. He can't even tell that the writing in front of him is in his own language.

Outside, the rains are turning the dirt path that runs by their shack into a river, but inside I detect a subtle change in Maynor's tone: one of confidence and pride. He is not the same kid he was a week ago when he left Tiquisate, and now his brain is hard at work thinking of what his life could become if he returns to Antigua and accepts Judy's offer to pay for his schooling.

۞

Judy isn't going to reach Traverse City tonight. Bad weather is making it nearly impossible to travel anywhere in the Western Hemisphere as one hurricane after another slams into the Gulf of Mexico this season, unleashing heavy winds and torrents of rain all the way from the Panama Canal to Canada. Millions of Indian peasants in Central America and Mexico who have built their makeshift homes on hilly inclines are praying that the rain gods don't wash away everything they own. Not even the mighty United States has been able to withstand the forces of nature. The dikes couldn't hold back Lake Pontchartrain and now New Orleans is flooded, and for weeks hundreds of millions of Americans have been grappling with horrific images of their countrymen, mostly poor and black, waiting on the roofs of their homes for helicopters that will never come—laying bare a systemic racism that Americans wanted to believe was in the past. Though the United States is considered a wealthy country, many of Hurricane Katrina's victims are as impoverished and desperate as Antonia and her boys.

At midnight Judy curls up on a bench at the airport in Minneapolis, a regional Northwest Airlines hub to which her flight from Detroit was rerouted. She is completely exhausted, but all she can think about are Ellie and Maynor, these two bright and beautiful siblings who ended up with totally different lives. Though she knows the sentiment is elitist, she wishes she could have brought Maynor back with her, for she knows that, home in Michigan, she could keep him out of harm's way and he could go to school and smile all day long and be a big brother to Ellie all over again.

Maybe she and Bob should tell Ellie right away and take her down to Guatemala for spring break, if not sooner. "Who am I kidding?" Judy says out loud. "I can't keep this secret that long." She also worries about Antonia and how long the poor woman will live. I'm sure she has serious health issues and problems with her uterus, Judy tells herself, remembering the woman complaining of her chronic stomach problems. And the number of men she's slept with . . . Who knows what diseases she may have. I'd better not wait until Ellie finishes high school or speaks fluent Spanish. Antonia might not live that long.

She calls Bob on her cell phone and voices her doubts, and as he always does, he listens patiently and suggests that they mull over it for a while. "There's no hurry here. The girls don't suspect anything. They think you've been at the trade show in Indianapolis the last week and a half. Just try and get some sleep."

Sometime in the middle of the night, while Judy is dozing on a bench in the Minneapolis airport and I am safely back in Antigua, is when the mud slides break loose all over Guatemala, burying thousands alive and washing away bridges and entire stretches of highway.

❧

From the safe haven of Antigua, I don't immediately realize the gravity of the situation unfolding around me—death and destruction throughout much of Guatemala. I am already walking out the door of the hotel the next morning with my backpack strapped to my shoulders to depart for the western highland city of Quetzaltenango when Christian, the hotel manager, asks me if I'm nuts. "Do you plan on walking all the way there, Jacob? There are no roads open to the west. Mud slides have destroyed both highways, and no one should be leaving Antigua for days."

"Hunker down, grab a cup of coffee, and stay a few more days."

And so I become a refugee of sorts, stuck in the dizzying comfort of Antigua for several weeks, waiting patiently for word that the highways have reopened and talking to Judy on the telephone every other day about Antonia and Maynor's well-being and the impending decision of whether to tell Ellie that we have opened the door to her past. Judy must have caught a bug or eaten a parasite sometime during her ten days in Guatemala, for she falls ill the moment she arrives back in Michigan, and within a week she feels so dehydrated that she checks into the hospital for an IV injection. She can't get Guatemala out of her mind, or her body.

The *Prensa Libre* runs a photo on Thursday, October 6, two days after Judy's departure, of a spot on the Pacific highway, the all-important trade route to Mexico, where a bridge was literally lifted off its foundation by oncoming waters and washed away. Meanwhile, landslides from above have torn sections one hundred feet long from the winding, mountain-navigating Central American Highway, cutting western Guatemala off from its northern neighbor completely. President Berger declares a state of disaster, and the newspaper's editorial declares Hurricane Stan worse than Hurricane Mitch, which brought Central America to its knees in the fall of 1998.

By Friday, more than a thousand Guatemalans have been reported *desaparecido*. The word *disappeared* has an ominous meaning in this country, for it often refers to the tens of thousands who were officially "disappeared" during the civil war. Translation: their corpses were left by the military in shallow mass graves.

Shocking news emerges of an entire village called Panabáj on the shores of Lago de Atitlán all but wiped off the map by the mud slides that arrived early in the morning. Days of heavy rain pried loose enough land near the apex of Volcán San Lucas to unleash the murderer on a sprint down the side of the volcano, picking up speed as it descended, gobbling up trees and earth in its path. Hundreds of Tz'utuhil Mayan Indians sleeping soundly in their brick- and tin-walled huts probably didn't even hear the invader; those who saw the mud slides arrive like flash floods certainly had no time to escape unless they were already on the second story of one of the few buildings, like the schoolhouse or the police station, that remain standing.

The survivors of Panabáj spend days digging into the new layer of earth to recover the bodies of their friends and loved ones until President Berger himself arrives by helicopter in a show of solidarity, and the mayor of the village halts the recovery effort for fear that a cholera epidemic is breaking out. On October 9 the *New York Times* even runs a story about the community-wide search for the body of a four-year-old girl named Ana Castro Guzmán, as if recovering her corpse will somehow alleviate the suffering.

All tourists are forced to abandon their bohemian lifestyles and evacuate the villages around Lago de Atitlán. Weeks will pass before tourism returns to this region that depends on gringos buying Mayan weavings and other knickknacks as its primary livelihood. And months will pass before I am able to pay a visit to Panabáj, one of the many martyrs of Hurricane Stan, and walk on the swath of crusty barren earth as wide as a football field where hundreds of people were buried. A single cross and a wreath of flowers have been placed in the middle of this open, moonlike surface, and when I look straight up at Volcán San Lucas I can see an ugly brown snake slithering down the mountain through the green foliage until it opens up to nature's graveyard: the path of the mud slide.

༚

By Saturday, October 8, I am tired of killing time in Antigua, which has been an island of calm and prosperity surrounded by a sea of chaos in civil war and postwar Guatemala. I feel as impatient as the dozens of American couples, whom I see scattered at each nice hotel in town, waiting for their babies' paperwork to be processed so they can return to the United States as adoptive parents. I meet such a couple almost every day, it seems, in the Parque Central, or at the fine breakfast joint Doña Luisa's, named after the Mayan princess who was given as a gift to the Guatemalan conqueror, Pedro de Alvarado, and who returned to live in Antigua after Alvarado died. The conversations between the adopting parents and me usually unfold in the same manner. I help them order something from the menu in Spanish and tell them about my research on Guatemalan adoption, and they marvel at the beauty of this town while telling me their paperwork status in PGN before they can take their baby home with them.

I have been reading the newspapers all week in disbelief, and I am ready to witness genuine suffering, so on Saturday I throw on my grubbiest clothes and join Christian, the hotel manager, and a team of volunteers to help dig out a nearby village called Jocotenango, which was hit hard by the mud slides, though no one died. We arrive at 9:00 a.m. with purified water, bread, corn, and other vegetables and use the house of a guy named Jorge as our base for supplying food. Half of our team cooks soup in a huge vat and parks a pickup truck in the middle of the only street not inundated by mud so that it can serve as the focal point for two different food-supply lines. Meanwhile, Christian and I join the other half of the team and descend into the village with the few shovels and brooms made available to us to begin lifting and pushing the two feet of mud in every home out into the street, where the rain is still falling, albeit in a sprinkle now, and where every footpath has become a roaring river.

At noon we stop for lunch and help facilitate the supply line, which runs smoothly until one of the other villagers accuses Jorge of stealing the food that we hauled into his kitchen hours earlier. Heated words, and a fistfight breaks out, and though the police and military both have uniformed representatives standing just yards away, it is up to us, the gringos, to stop the scuffle. Someone reaches in and pulls Jorge off his victim, whose nose is bleeding, and asks him why the hell he's fighting with his own villagers when Mother Nature just looked down and, with a snap of her fingers, killed thousands of his countrymen and turned rural Guatemala into a soupy mess.

The fight ends, and we eat our lunch and return to the houses most filled with mud. But the river outside in the street is rising, and if we don't divert or get rid of the water completely, the houses will reflood and all our work in the morning will be wasted. So a few German amateur engineers and I decide to dig several big holes at the base of the street in what once was someone's garden, to drain the water. And that's where we are, in sandals, up to our knees in muddy water that could quite possibly be contaminated, when we hear the gunshots.

Jorge's nephew, it seems, has taken exception to the insults hurled at his uncle. The man opens his home for emergency food supplies for the whole village, and someone accuses him of being a thief? That's not right at all! So the young man gets himself all worked up and shows up at our cleanup site looking for the perpetrator. But the guy with the bloody nose dented by Jorge is gone, so the nephew picks out a tiny peasant man who has been working alongside us all day and fires four warning shots over his tiny head, at point-blank range from across the stream, yelling at him all the while. Christian stands right next to the kid with the gun, and I am about thirty feet away, and we are both convinced we are about to see our first execution.

Thankfully, the nephew calms down, or he just realizes he has the wrong man. Or maybe he turns and gazes up at the mountain towering behind him that unleashed the mud slides earlier this week and realizes the irony of what he is doing. I think of the scene in Vonnegut's *Slaughterhouse Five* when the German soldier executes the American prisoner of war for stealing a teapot in the middle of empty, firebombed Dresden. In any case, Jorge's nephew returns the gun to the back pocket of his jeans and walks away.

The policemen and military team just around the bend at the food-supply line hear the shots, but don't come running or even do a thing. Only when Christian and I confront them, and, ignoring that we must look like primeval beings having just risen from the bog and that they carry AK-47s in their arms, we yell at them to arrest the idiot with the gun. Only then do they wander off and pretend to look for the shooter.

Less out of fear for our own safety and more out of anger with the villagers for fighting among themselves in the middle of a natural disaster, we pack up and leave for Antigua. Sitting in the back of the pickup truck the whole ride back into town I feel furious with these people for sinking to such a level when we are trying to help, and I vow not to help any more mud-slide victims, at least not in Jocotenango. Later that night at a favorite Antigua dive frequented more by locals than by tourists, I find someone who shares my rage. "Mierda Guatemala," replies the bartender named Chavo after hearing my story. "Only in Guatemala. Fucking Guatemala."

On that same day a massive earthquake hits a remote region of Pakistan, killing tens of thousands instantly, and the attention span of the Western world that can focus for only so long on regions outside its borders, and usually only one place at a time, naturally shifts to Asia, and Hurricane Stan's effects on Guatemala are mostly forgotten. But not by everyone.

In Michigan, the way Ellie learns that her adoptive mother, Judy, has met her biological mother, Antonia, is anticlimactic and comical, typical of a minidrama involving American teenage sisters. Judy can't keep the secret any longer; she tells one of the twins, sixteen-year-old Amelia, on Friday, October 14, on the condition that Ellie isn't to know. Naturally, Amelia tells Ellie that same night: "Mom wasn't in Indianapolis on her trip. She was in Guatemala, and she found your birth mother and your brothers. But you can't tell her that you know. I wasn't supposed to tell."

And when Judy finally spills the beans to Ellie the following day, the girl's immediate reaction is not one of joy or suspense or confusion, and the questions about her roots and her former life or when they can go visit don't spill out just yet. That is all to come. Ellie's first question to Judy is why Amelia was told first, and not her. The fourteen year old feels sorry for herself for about an hour, but no more. That's when she begins thinking about Guatemala and the reunion.

11 🌿 Reunion

Nothing more than a car window and a roadside gutter separate Ellie from the teenagers walking on the side of the highway, bent over in what looks like agony as they bear heavy bundles of sticks on their backs. A brother and sister in tattered clothing and worn-out sandals, probably about to begin a trek of several miles up into a remote village so their mother will have wood for cooking that night. The girl feels her load slipping, and the boy runs around behind her to provide support. Neither one looks up at the tourist minivan passing by, slowing down to pass gently over the bumps in the road, just long enough to give Ellie a look at this genuine moment of Guatemalan poverty. She doesn't turn off the American hip-hop music playing on her iPod, but it's clear she is taking a long, hard look at these two siblings trudging along on the side of the road—a life that might have been hers had she not been adopted six years earlier.

Today is Friday, February 3, 2006, Judy and Ellie's second full day in Guatemala after landing on Wednesday night. We traveled to Monterrico, a laid-back, touristy dive on the steamy Pacific coast yesterday so that mother and daughter could have a little fun before the big reunion tomorrow. Since Antonia, Maynor, and William have no money for transportation, I will wake up at dawn and catch a chicken bus for Tiquisate to pick them up and bring them back to Antigua for the moment that has haunted Ellie's dreams ever since she was abandoned. Despite the concerns of some of Judy's friends and family, she decided to bring Ellie down to Guatemala before the girl's fifteenth birthday, and even before Traverse City public schools let out for spring break in late March. Judy is worried about the biological mother's health, as Antonia battles constant pain in her uterus, and there is no way she'll let the woman die without giving Ellie a chance to meet her again. That grand moment is less than twenty-four hours away now, and none of the three of us quite knows how to deal with it. We are all terribly nervous.

Ellie turns off the Daddy Yankee track and looks across the seat toward me when I ask her what she thinks when she sees the poor kids working on the side of the road.

"When I see them it reminds me of when I was little and I lived like them. I see how lucky I am to be with a good family, living the good life." The teenager's quotes are often repetitive and clichéd, but they are certainly genuine. "I feel really bad for them that they don't have much fun and they always have to work. I just feel really, really lucky."

As she did yesterday, Ellie has painted her upper face with mascara and eyeliner, and that makes her look older than fourteen. She wears big silver earrings with three holes in them so they resemble smiling faces, and a stylish black sweatshirt that zips down in the middle, with the word *SHORTY* written across the chest. Judy tried to persuade Ellie to wear a T-shirt in Monterrico, given the coastal humidity, but the girl chose fashion first and scoffed at her mother when she tried to intervene and choose Ellie's wardrobe. She sweated under the tropical sun and refused to change because, Judy told me, Ellie is worried about her figure and that's why she prefers a baggy sweatshirt. "No, Mom, I just want to look cool," Ellie says during the bus ride.

Later that afternoon in Antigua, as we walk past the Parque Central and up the street of the yellow arch for dinner at the Fonda de la Calle Real, where Bill Clinton ate once during his second term as president, Ellie draws more than one stare and whistle from local boys. She is wearing brown short shorts and showing plenty of leg—something a fourteen-year-old girl might be able to get away with in the United States but seems suggestive in Guatemala because the kids hook up so young here. Judy tells me they had a mini fight while packing for their trip here. "My idea was to teach her what was appropriate to wear on a trip to another culture in another country, in order for her to blend in. But she only likes to wear shorts that are too short."

"I like to wear shorts because it's like summer here and at home it's always, like, winter, and I have to wear jeans there," Ellie retorts as the corn tamales wrapped in banana leaves, the traditional Guatemalan food she has dreamed about for years, arrive on the table.

"What do you think about tomorrow?" I ask Ellie. "Are you excited, nervous?"

"I'm mostly excited about seeing the reactions on their faces when I see them," Ellie says about tomorrow. Is she nervous? "I just want to get to know them."

"What are you most worried about?"

"Just what they will think when they see me. That's all. I'm just nervous."

So are we all, as we begin to realize the gravity of what will happen tomorrow and as the enormity sinks in. This is the culmination of Ellie's journey—a collision course between wealth and poverty, present and past, and it could wreak havoc on this fourteen-year-old girl. An event like this one looming over us has traditionally scared, or at least worried, many adoptive parents, according to adoption case workers as well as an American private investigator I met in the Parque Central in Antigua who tracks down birth mothers. They might interpret the reunion as a sign that their adopted child is rejecting them, or also for fear of the wounds that the experience may reopen.

Adopted children traditionally have not been given the right to track down and meet their biological mothers—a result of the birth mother's perceived right to privacy. But the movement of adopted children fighting for the right to know their biological mothers has achieved monumental victories, thanks to activists like Wayne Carp and organizations like Oregon-based Bastard Nation, which lobbies for all adoption records to be opened. The aforementioned American private investigator also believes that a recent wave of books and documentaries like Alex Haley's *Roots*—and more recently *Outsiders*

Within: Writing on Transracial Adoption—has prompted curiosity and longing in the hearts of thousands to research their past.

Interestingly, Betty Jean Lifton reports that most adoptees who seek their biological parents are women: "This would seem logical when we remember that it is the girls who ply their adoptive mothers with questions while growing up, as if concerned even then with the problems around biological continuity. Women are closer to their feelings. They are the ones who face becoming mothers themselves, and who yearn for some knowledge of that woman who went before them into the rites of childbirth—an experience they cannot share with their adoptive mothers."

Outside, clouds have formed a blanket over Antigua, and a few raindrops were felt earlier in the day, leaving wet cobblestones all across town, even though the rainy season ended here months ago. I look south and see occasional bolts of lightning striking over Volcán de Agua. What are the gods trying to tell us?

※

It is the next day, in the early afternoon, and we are walking east up 5 Calle toward the Parque Central, our feet looking out for loose cobblestones that could twist an ankle, our knees and hips sometimes jumping out of the way of three-wheeled Tuc-tuc taxis or cars speeding by, but our minds and hearts focusing on the sweet, mysterious moment that lies just a few blocks ahead, and minutes away. Maynor, seventeen, William, fifteen, and their two nephews, Mincho and Erik, eight and five, move at a brisk pace, and occasionally I have to corral them with my arms to let old, slow-moving Antonia, her boyfriend, Wagner, and her oldest daughter Maritza, twenty-seven, catch up. This is a family affair, and though I don't want to force anything to happen a certain way since I must remain true to my role as documentarian, I figure it's only fair if they all meet Ellie at the exact same time.

Maynor is dressed in his best clothing: a pressed white-collared dress shirt, black pants, and a shiny black belt—attire he must have purchased from the meager salary he's made picking bananas on the *finca* this last month since he quit the Safe Passage program in Antigua after only a few weeks and returned home to be with his girlfriend, Guadalupe, and quite possibly to marry her. Maynor's black hair is slicked back with gel, and he still wears the brown shoes that Judy bought him back in October of the previous year when she initially met the family, though they are nearly worn out by now. William has not yet met Judy, and he dresses casually, in a Nike soccer shirt, blue jeans, and an old gray sweatshirt hanging over his shoulders. Based on the wardrobes, it appears that this day means more to Maynor, and he is the one pressing the group of boys ahead of the pack. He is the one who was semiadopted by Judy in the fall, and then disappointed her by ditching school and returning to the impoverished village. He is the one who has written letters, and heard his long-lost sister's voice on the phone these past four months. The last time Maynor and William saw Ellie, who was Berenice then, was seven years ago when they chased the car with the girl looking out the back window, trying to stop their sister from being taken away from them. But today it is Maynor, more than anyone, pushing ahead, skimming across the loose cobblestones like a bicycle, to do what would have been impossible just a few months ago—to meet his sister again.

At the Parque Central we turn south, walking away from the yellow arch where Judy and Ellie and I had dinner the night before and toward Volcán de Agua. Mincho and Erik hold the hands of Maynor and William as they feel the anticipation begin to take hold inside their little bellies, and Antonia, Wagner, and Maritza walk about ten paces behind. Antonia wears a pink blouse that once hung loose but now wraps tight around her body. She has on a brown-and-white skirt that I haven't seen before and sandals. When I called her from Chicago the week before and told her that Judy and Ellie would arrive within days and that, at long last, they could meet the girl again, she whooped with joy over the phone, and gone was the voice of anguish tormented by the constant pain in her stomach. Still, Antonia is in terrible physical shape, and no matter how badly she wants to, she can't pick up her pace in anticipation of seeing Ellie.

The family and I have already eaten lunch at a corner steak grill and checked into rooms at a budget hotel, so they could store their belongings before the eight-block walk. I thought this reunion might not be as exciting for Maritza's two little ones. Since Erik is only five, he's never met Ellie, so I didn't want to force them through this on empty stomachs. This day has already been long and intense. But ever since I arrived at Maritza's house, where Antonia and the boys now live too, next to the old torn-up United Fruit Company train tracks outside the village near Tiquisate called Rio Bravo, I have absorbed the rays of happiness and good fortune on the faces of these characters, and that has calmed my own nerves.

The cobblestone street becomes smooth as we pass by several wealthy homes and hotels in this more residential area of Antigua, and the expensive BMWs and sport utility vehicles parked along the side of the road boast a lacquered shine. We pass a wine bar on the right and the fancy Panza Verde restaurant on the left, and Agua looms larger and larger in front of us. The sky is partly cloudy, but the sun shines down on this entourage and it's a warm day in Antigua. The gods above appear tranquil today.

There, I see a door on the left side of the street open, waiting for us. La Capilla is a quaint hotel run by two Canadian women, with a pool and a sunroof, where the hipsters and artists of Antigua often come for afternoon cocktails. This is where Judy and Ellie are waiting, inside. The moment of reckoning is nearly upon us.

❧

It all happens so quickly that without my 2.0 Megapixel Nikon Coolpix camera in hand, capable of shooting a digital photo every three or four seconds, I will never be able to capture the details of exactly what will transpire when Eleanor Patricia Berenice Ortiz is reunited with her birth mother who, out of poverty, desperation, and outside pressure, gave her up all those years ago.

Judy and Ellie are not in the courtyard when we enter, and, wary of the emotional scene about to unfold by the pool in front of sun-starved tourists, I ask the Guatemalan family to wait in the entrance while I go and find mother and daughter. And there, at the end of the hallway leading from the pool, I come face-to-face with Ellie, her radiant long dark hair hanging down over her left shoulder and her face breaking into a wide smile when she sees me. Dressed in a denim jacket and stylish new dark jeans, she looks absolutely beautiful, and happy. The sunlight over the pool and the bright-pink walls behind her form a great contrast in the photo between darkness and light.

"There are some people here to see you, Ellie," I say, as she blushes. "They've been waiting quite a while."

And when I turn and take four steps back to the stone courtyard with Ellie following behind me and to my left, the first person we see is Antonia, standing frozen in place, frozen in time. In the photo she is rubbing her belly with her right hand and clenching part of the pink blouse, maybe out of the anxiety of the moment, or maybe because here was where she bore this girl. Antonia's face looks melancholy, her eyes already moist, and yes, she seems to be gazing off to the left, toward Ellie. She sees her: the girl she loved but gave up for peer pressure, for hope, for money she would never receive; the girl she tried to reclaim weeks later but was defeated by the lawyers, retreating to El Salvador to mourn her loss.

Antonia takes one step, maybe two, but it is Ellie who rushes forward and embraces her mother, the girl's arms clasping her neck and Antonia wrapping her right arm around Ellie's neck and her left around Ellie's waist, pulling close to her the girl she never thought she'd see again. Both of their long dark tails of hair cascade down their backs, making the photo strangely symmetrical. As I move to a different angle I see that Antonia is crying hard now and holding Ellie tighter and tighter.

A moment later Judy appears, and she and Antonia join in a half embrace, all the while looking at Ellie, the sun shining fully on the girl's happy face now. Ellie has stepped back, her right hand propped under her left elbow and her left hand playing with her bangs. She stares at her two mothers and smiles wide. Her life is complete at this moment—the hole in her heart filled.

William joins the celebration and meets Judy for the first time, making it a circle. Both Judy and Antonia continue to hold onto Ellie's waist as she runs her fingers through her hair and eyes her brother. Oh, but where is Maynor, the leader of the procession to meet Ellie, the one who accompanied Antonia on that day Judy and I showed up in Tiquisate, the de facto man of the house once their father, Esvin, split?

Maynor is leaning behind a post near the doorway so that no one can see him sobbing, afraid that Ellie will see her older brother in this state perhaps. I finally yell, "Maynor, come over here! Come meet your sister!" Judy and Antonia join in, but once again it is Ellie who walks over and meets him two-thirds of the way to the post, where he never stops crying but opens his brotherly arms to embrace her and won't let her go for minutes. Maynor buries his face in Ellie's right shoulder, his nose nuzzling her hair, inevitably creating a wet spot on her denim jacket, and to anyone at La Capilla lucky enough to witness it, this particular reunion between sister and brother must seem like the most intimate, joyous one of all.

When the five-minute hug finally ends, Maynor is still sobbing, though faintly, and Ellie's smile is still as wide as ever. This stoic young woman has yet to shed a single tear.

༠

By and by, Judy ushers us upstairs onto the sunny roof where she has prearranged a special treat: a waiter serves us seviche shrimp salad followed by soft drinks and snacks, and I place my blue tape recorder on the wooden table next to the pile of napkins and containers of hot sauce and ketchup and let the tape roll, to pick up the organic sounds of an abandoned girl being reacquainted with her lost family.

"I feel so happy because she returned to see us," Antonia opens the dialogue. "I thought she was lost forever." The birth mother's voice trails off as she begins to sob uncontrollably.

And after that a long silence follows. No one in the family has the courage, or the need, to say anything, and the thought passes through my head that the scene is almost anticlimactic.

Antonia has to get Ellie's attention to pass her a plastic cup of Coke. The girl seems stuck in a daydream, but a good one, and she doesn't respond right away. Judy explains that Ellie was awake by seven this morning and felt so confused and anxious that she couldn't make decisions all day. She would order a drink and then refuse it. She wanted a haircut, and then didn't want a haircut. She hasn't eaten anything until now.

"Why isn't anyone talking?" I ask.

"No hay palabras," Antonia replies. There are no words for this.

"Has anything changed about her?" I ask Antonia, pointing to Ellie.

"Nada. She's the same girl I remember."

The gathering breaks into smaller conversations, smaller threads. Wagner's cell phone rings, and he walks off to answer it. Alex, the Canadian hostess, brings more seviche. Judy teaches William how to say "I love you" in English.

Antonia begins to mumble about Esvin, the father of her children, and how he kicked her out of the house for another woman. He and Esperanza have another little girl named Glendy who is five years old and looks a little like Ellie, she tells us.

I ask Antonia what she told Ellie when they first embraced.

"I told her, 'You're a beautiful girl, and it's wonderful to see you again after seven years.' But I gave you up so you would be well, so you would have opportunities that you wouldn't have had with me. With me you would have suffered. We have gone hungry so often." The poor woman begins to weep again, and Maritza fills in.

"She has suffered lots with her kids. They have had to move from one place to the next when she couldn't find work, living from day to day."

Judy jumps in. "I say thank you every day to Antonia for giving life to Ellie, because she's a fantastic girl. She's so talented; she sings well, paints well . . ."

Antonia interrupts, and through her sniffles: "I never thought I'd see this day. I thought I'd lost you forever."

Judy asks Ellie if there's anything she'd like to say to her biological mother.

"I just want to tell her that this is my dream come true."

Antonia rehashes how much she regrets lying to Ellie when she took her to the orphanage here in Antigua and gave her up, how she felt manipulated by Cesy, and later the lawyer Cassandra. She looks at Ellie, takes the girl's hand, and tells her that she returned to Antigua to ask the powers that be if she could see her daughter, but they wouldn't let her. She returned to Tiquisate and asked Estela, the other intermediary, for help, but again she was refused.

The tears are streaming down Antonia's face now, yet this is her monologue. All eyes and ears are focused on her, and there are no understudies waiting backstage.

For support, Judy adds, "And yet they told me at Hogar Nuevo Día that Ellie cried for three weeks straight after she arrived there."

"I just didn't want my daughter to suffer with me, because Esvin took my house and threw us out onto the street. I gave up the other four too because I didn't want them to suffer."

Antonia pauses and takes a bite of her seviche. "She isn't upset that I gave her up?" Antonia asks the crowd, though nodding toward Ellie.

"She's not the only one." Ellie pops out of her trance in reply, not just to Antonia but to her brothers and sister, and Judy and me. "A lot of people here give up their children for adoption, because of the poverty here . . . I forgive her."

And so the dark veil is lifted, and the mood all around suddenly lightens. The heavy words have been exchanged, and all are forgiven for their sins of the past. Hot and sweaty under the sun overhead, Maynor takes off his white dress shirt, and one of the little ones runs up and squeezes his left nipple for a laugh. Antonia takes a second helping of seviche, and she and Maritza begin to reminisce about the easier days before Ellie was given up.

Maritza remembers a little red dress that Ellie would always put on before prancing around in front of the mirror. The older sister would tell her to stop admiring herself, and the two would fight. Antonia tells Ellie about her own mother, seventy years old and still alive in rural El Salvador. "Chepa," as they call her, has a beautiful voice, and she would take Ellie to church with her back in the old days to sing. Judy's eyes light up. That explains her natural voice talent.

Meanwhile, the English-language lessons begin. Ellie tells her brothers that her last name is "Walters," and the Guatemalans fall all over themselves trying to pronounce it. "Woy-ters" . . . William gets the closest, to rousing laughter. Next Judy teaches Maynor and William to say the word *girlfriend*, though the flat American *r* sound is impossible for these boys to pronounce. I turn to Ellie and teach her to say in Spanish, "Mis hermanos se llaman William y Maynor." Maynor finds this game so funny he sits down and bounces his forehead on his knee, while William leans forward on the balls of his feet, licks his fingers, and runs them through his hair to look suave.

Someone notices that William and Ellie each have a tiny scar in the exact same place above their right eye. Antonia remembers each separate incident. William was playing with a bigger kid near a river, and he was pushed in and hit his head on a rock. Ellie was at a neighbor's house jumping on beds with her brothers. She tried to jump from one bed to the next but didn't clear the hurdle. She fell to the ground and hit her head and bit her tongue open. It bled a whole lot, Antonia remembers. Sure enough, Ellie opens her mouth and sticks out her tongue to show us the scar.

As the mood lightens and the conversation turns toward the ordinary, I decide my documenting and translating skills are no longer needed, so I retire to a hammock several yards away for a snooze. But before drifting off I notice them: William in a catcher's crouch near the ground, Antonia seated with her left arm on his shoulder as she hovers over him, and Maynor seated to her right stroking her ponytail, which is pulled together in a leopard-print bow tie. What a loving family. Meanwhile, Ellie is seated to Maynor's right with a look of silent contentment. Maybe she notices the same thing too.

Minutes later—or is it an hour later?—I open my eyes and see

Maynor and Ellie moving the plastic tables over to the outer edge of the roof in silence, helping each other. They walk back to the group, each rubbing their hands together as if in synch . . . like brother and sister.

૨₹

When I finally wake up from my nap I find I am alone on the roof, gazing down beside the pool at Antigua's young, artsy hipsters laughing, drinking cocktails, and smoking cigarettes next to their reflections in the azure water. I walk downstairs and open the sliding glass door into Judy and Ellie's room, and I see them—the entire family, Guatemalans and gringos alike, snuggled up together on the queen-size bed as if Ellie had never been torn apart from her mother and brothers in the first place. At the head of the bed on the right side, Maritza has her arms wrapped around Antonia's stomach from behind, rubbing it. Antonia is in the middle, and only inches away from her is Judy, still asleep (or maybe her eyes just shut when my camera flash goes off), but best of all, at the foot of the bed are Ellie, Maynor, and William all lying on their stomachs. The boys take turns listening to the hip-hop music on Ellie's iPod.

Any doubts that the three siblings have already rebuilt their strong bonds dissipate by Saturday evening. Maynor, William, Ellie, Antonia, Wagner, Maritza, Erik, Mincho, Judy, and I dine in a private section of a little restaurant with a dance floor and mirrors on three sides called Chimenos, and after dinner Ellie leads her brothers in a series of hip-hop dance moves as Daddy Yankee, the Puerto Rican godfather of Reggaeton music, pumps through the speakers. "Le gusta la gasolina," he pronounces. "Da me más gasolina," the divas answer. Ellie claps her hands together and sways her hips back and forth like a high school dance-team cheerleader back in the States. Maynor and William, and the little ones, Mincho and Erik, line up behind her, eager to learn.

When their turn in front of the camera arrives, Maynor and William show Ellie they know how to break dance, and she looks on in delight and pride at the athleticism and beauty of her older brothers.

"They are so cool." Ellie's eyes seem to reflect what she's thinking, and I realize while shooting dozens of digital pictures from across the dance floor that this is their true reunion, and not the moment of first contact or the awkward dialogue over seviche this afternoon. It is really now that Maynor, William, and Berenice are together again, playing the way they did in the old days.

A language barrier may separate them from engaging in profound dialogue, since Ellie has forgotten almost all of her Spanish and understands only the simplest things Maynor and William tell her. Still, this evening hand gestures, smiles, and dance moves will suffice.

𝔞𝔨

But as Judy told Ellie on Friday night over dinner, the reunion would not last forever, and at some point the girl will have to say good-bye to her Guatemalan family, for a time at least, and return to the United States to continue her studies. There at the Fonda de la Calle Real, the night before the reunion, the adoptive mother asked the adopted daughter if she could handle that—saying good-bye to her roots once again.

"What if they are to say, 'Stop being a gringa'? 'Stop living there and come back and live in Tiquisate now'? How would that make you feel? I mean, I don't think they are going to say that, but . . ."

"I don't know," Ellie answered with hesitation.

"Do you think you'd feel strong enough?" Judy continued. "There are also safety issues that Dad talked about. What if someone says, 'Get into this taxi and let's go'?"

"I'm not that stupid, Mom."

And Judy had no reason to think that would happen, and so she dropped the subject.

The good-bye would unfold in phases, the first one happening a day after the reunion on Sunday afternoon. Judy decided that Ellie should have some time alone with her brothers before Maynor had to return to work on the banana *finca* on Wednesday morning, and so she suggested that Antonia, Wagner, Maritza, and the two little ones leave on a bus for Tiquisate in the afternoon, to make it easier for Ellie.

The entire family gathers for breakfast at a restaurant across from the budget hotel where the Guatemalans stayed the night before, and Antonia and her boys all order the exact same meal as Judy and I, a show of respect. We march around past the bus terminal to a private hospital called Hermano Pedro where Judy pays a doctor to examine Antonia and her stomach problems. "I saw her urine in our toilet last night," she whispers to me. "It was filled with blood." The doctor concurs with Judy and doesn't need a second look to determine that the ailing woman should have a hysterectomy. Her uterus should be removed.

But poor Antonia winces in fright at the thought of a knife carving into her, and when we meet the rest of the family back on the street and share the prognosis with them, she begins to weep. The Guatemalans all oppose surgery, telling Judy that the pills and occasional shots her doctor in Tiquisate prescribed for her will do the trick. Maynor and Maritza both corner me as we walk back to the bus terminal and tell me that the doctors at the public hospital in Tiquisate, where the operation would be all but free, are evil. They don't know what they are doing, and often people die from surgery and are cast out onto the street afterward. Of course, I know medical procedures are much more complicated than that, but I decide not to reply. I remember how Antonia sought out the Evangelical healer to cure the witchcraft that she thought was ailing her instead of paying money for modern medicine.

How far apart this family is in mind and soul from the world Judy and Ellie know. The girl is still mostly silent today as she walks across the cobblestones with her brothers. Does Ellie see how fragile and scared her biological mother really is, and what that's doing to her, knowing she has to say good-bye once again?

We still have a half hour before the 3:00 p.m. chicken bus to Escuintla departs down the street in front of the bus terminal, and so Judy offers to take Antonia and Maritza shopping in the Antigua market, with Ellie, of course, a girls' excursion. They quickly discover that beans and rice cost much more here than they do in Tiquisate, so Judy gives the women cash instead of buying them gifts, and they return to meet the rest of us on the Calzado Santa Lucia, precious minutes before the departure hour.

The family mingles on the sidewalk in a carefree spirit, joking and laughing as if the family's problems are all in the past. Suddenly, William yells out that the bus to Escuintla is here, and I run out into the street to flag it down.

And from there the carefully planned reunion slips into painful chaos, as I realize that poor Ellie will be forced to say good-bye to Antonia literally on the run. True to form, the chicken-bus driver slows to a creep but refuses to stop completely, and I run up the steps and yell at him to stop. I walk out in front of the bus, hold up my open-palmed right hand like a traffic cop, and then turn to my left and watch in horror as Ellie refuses to let go of her biological mother, the tears streaming from her eyes now. On the same street, seven years later, a scene is unfolding not all that dissimilar from the day Ellie was relinquished. Only the one being escorted onto the bus is the mother, not the daughter.

Antonia finally breaks away and sobs loving words to Berenice, mysteriously now a part of her life again, and she follows Wagner, Maritza, Mincho, and Erik onto the bus. I move out of the driver's way, and as the chicken bus begins to roll forward we see Antonia this time, pressing her face against a window and waving good-bye to Ellie, her face quickly becoming smaller as the bus picks up speed. But this time no one chases after it.

Instead, Maynor, William, Ellie, Judy, and I turn and walk the other way, toward the Parque Central. The three siblings move ahead of us and look completely dejected. Ellie is beside herself for the first time during her reunion, crying and locked in an embrace with Maynor, who holds her and whispers comforting words to her in a language that only siblings can understand. The brother and sister are mourning for their mother, her departure, her ill health, and for the ultimate good-bye that Judy has told them will come on Tuesday. Their unity is hauntingly beautiful despite its anguish.

Invisible to us, a profound bond is embedding itself deep inside their bones.

12 ﴾ Escape

Monday evening, the day after Antonia returns to Tiquisate and the day before Ellie will say good-bye to her brothers, is a very important dinner date. Hanley Denning, the founder of Safe Passage who befriended Judy when she came to Traverse City, Michigan, the previous fall to speak about the horrible conditions for kids growing up in the Guatemala City garbage dump, is to meet us at 6:30 in the Parque Central and discuss the possibility of readmitting Maynor into the program if he so desires, and maybe even William too. Hanley was equally heartbroken in early January when Maynor refused to return to Antigua to begin school and pledged his intent to marry his girlfriend, Guadalupe. But now Judy thinks there is a good chance that Maynor will change his mind and consent to returning to school once he sees Hanley.

Five minutes before our meeting I arrive at the water fountain in the *parque* and find Judy, who is visibly baffled because she hasn't seen Maynor, William, or Ellie. They were up on the roof of the hotel La Capilla, or in the pool down below most of the day, playing and looking upbeat. So where are those little rascals? We agree that Judy will return to the hotel to check once again and ask Alex, the manager, to send them to the coffee bar at the edge of the *parque* where Hanley and I will be waiting before dinner.

The concerned mother returns fifteen minutes later and finds Hanley, another Safe Passage employee, and me, only to report that there is no sign of the kids. No reason to worry, we all tell Judy. They certainly wouldn't leave Antigua. Maynor is probably just afraid of meeting

Hanley because he's indecisive about his future, and he's embarrassed that he let her down in the first place. We order Judy an espresso, and I jog down the street to the budget hotel where Maynor and William are staying to ask the manager if he's seen them. Again, no sign.

What can we do? the four of us think. If Maynor doesn't want to be pressured to go to school in Antigua, he and his brother and sister will hide out until later in the evening and then come back to the hotel when the temperature drops. We can't force him to do anything. If they want to play hide-and-seek, let them do it. Haven't we all done it at one time or another?

Judy, Hanley, her colleague Rachel, and I move to an Italian restaurant just around the corner from the coffee bar after letting the baristas know to send them over to us. Still convinced that they will show up, Judy orders a large ham and pepperoni pizza for the kids and us to split. She tries to eat but her stomach is tied in nervous knots. What if something has happened to them? This is Guatemala, after all, and the bodies of teenage boys and girls show up on city streets almost every day, sometimes mutilated, sometimes raped.

Judy manages to chew a couple of pieces, but never before in her life has freshly cooked pizza felt so hard to digest. She can't imagine that they would try to escape, especially given the respect she has from Maynor and William after all she's done for their family lately. And that's what we all reaffirm to Judy. But inside of her the doubts are growing. She knew that Maynor especially, but William as well, was not looking forward to saying good-bye to Ellie tomorrow, even though she has said many times during this sweet reunion that their relationship is just beginning anew.

At eight Judy and Hanley walk back to La Capilla once more to hear if Alex has any news, but also to see if any money is missing from Judy's suitcase. The door was left unlocked, and Ellie would have known where to find the stash. No news from Alex, and the cash is all still there. But wait, one of the actors rehearsing in the lobby at La Capilla does remember seeing the three kids walk out the front door, between five thirty and six, he guesses. Judy thinks back to the last time she saw them, which would have been around that same time, when she was sitting on a lounge chair by the pool reading a dramatic paperback novel and Maynor came down from the roof to ask if he could borrow my cellular phone to call Antonia. Five minutes, he was told, no more, and he returned with the phone four minutes later.

By nine Judy finds herself on the verge of tears, and waiting patiently, hoping the kids will return, is no longer an option. How can any mother sit still when she has reason to worry that something terrible has happened to her child? We try to deflect her impulses, knowing that they won't do any good. Calling Bob will just make him worried sick too, especially since he's far away and can't do a thing. And asking the Guatemalan police for help is always a pointless gesture. "They're here in town somewhere, Judy, I guarantee you," I tell her.

By nine thirty Judy calls Bob from my cell phone and leaves a message: "Ellie has gone missing. So have the boys." I cringe when I think of what he will think, and do, when he presses "Play" on the answering machine and listens to his wife's desperate, quivering voice. At ten I give in again, and we file a missing-person report with both the Antigua police and the tourist police. Judy needs to feel she is doing something to find her daughter, and at least this will keep us busy for a little while. "Three teenage Guatemalan kids in hooded sweatshirts," I tell the police. "The girl doesn't speak Spanish, but the boys do. They may be leading the way, but I don't want anything to happen to them, either." Judy and I jump into a squad car, and we patrol up and down a few dark streets. Antigua is cold and windy this time of night.

"Where do you want me to look?" the policeman asks.

"I don't know. What do you usually do?"

"Usually we don't send out a search party until the person has been missing for a couple of days . . . Wait, you said the girl is their sister? So then what's the problem? She probably left with them willingly . . ."

Realizing that a police patrol is pointless, we call up Antonia and Maritza, initially just to check in and hear how their return trip went the day before, and fishing for signs of information about the kids.

But it's late, and when the phone rings after ten o'clock they know something must be up. We don't hide anything. "Ellie and the boys are missing. We haven't seen them since this afternoon. Do you have any idea where they might be?"

"Missing! *Ay no*," Antonia exclaims in a state of shock. "It's cold this time of night in Antigua. I'm worried about them out all alone."

"So you haven't heard from them?"

"No, no." Her voice seems shocked.

"What about Wagner—where is he?"

"He's in Santa Lucia, at his sister's place. Maritza didn't want him to live with us in the house, so he's out there, in the jungle."

Suddenly, Maritza's voice speaks on the other end. "Listen, we are going to call Wagner and find out if he knows anything about where they are. If I can't get hold of him, I'll go there tomorrow morning. But call me back in ten minutes."

We do so, and Maritza relays the chilling news.

❧

"Vamos a escapar con Berenice" were the words Maynor used when he called Wagner on my cell phone late in the afternoon. "We're going to escape with Berenice. I don't want her to go."

The older brother asked his little sister up on the roof at La Capilla if she really wanted to go back to the United States on Thursday and leave them here, again. It was a leading question, no doubt.

"No, I don't want to go," she replied, and the fuse was lit. It was complicit.

Maynor returned to the pool to bring me back my cell phone and avoided saying or doing anything that would raise suspicion. "The coast is clear," he would have told William and Berenice, for that is who she is now. "Judy is reading a book by the pool . . . Let's go!"

Sometime between five thirty and six they sneaked behind us, into the lobby and out through the front door, bounding like jackrabbits through Antigua's streets as evening approached and the setting sun cast an orange glow over the walls of houses and the sky above. They were together again and free, these three siblings. They would defy the world, defy all logic, and, as long as they could manage it, never be separated again.

Maynor has a secret stash of money he earned while working in the banana *fincas*, and he was probably saving it for an opportunity like this. He won't let the gringos take away his dear sister again. He's going to outsmart them. Down a couple of side streets he leads his siblings. Maynor had ample time to get to know the layout of Antigua during his week here with Judy and me and his brief stint at Safe Passage in December. He knows an alternate route to the highway leaving Antigua for Escuintla, and there they jump on a chicken bus heading south, into the dangerous night, for the southern coast.

They huddle together as they descend toward the coastal lowlands, through the fields of sugarcane and bananas that Maynor and William know so well. To the girl's great disappointment, Judy wasn't going to let Ellie see Tiquisate this time around because she thought it was too dangerous, and Maynor knows this. Some would say he is manipulating his sister; others would call this nothing more than a childish prank. "Don't you want to go and see our home, Bereníce? It's nice and hot, and our entire family will be happy to see you again. You can come and live with us in our house by the railroad tracks, and you can meet my beautiful girlfriend, Guadalupe." How could Bereníce say no to that?

On the chicken bus, squeezed safely between her two caring and brave brothers, she thinks briefly about how Judy will react when she realizes they are gone. Will she be angry or disappointed? Will she come and try to find me, or will she go back to Michigan alone? Oh, but Bereníce is so excited to see Tiquisate again, and spend more time with Antonia, and play with Maynor and William, her beautiful, athletic brothers. She shouldn't have to be separated from them again: it just isn't fair.

Poor Bereníce has come face-to-face with the family she lost, and in just three days she has rekindled a deep bond with them. Some of Bereníce's Spanish has returned since Saturday, and now she understands much of what her brothers tell her, though her own vocabulary is still very limited. Last night, for instance, Maynor walked her through the menu at a Greek restaurant where we ate dinner, helping her pronounce the tough words in Spanish and roll her *r*'s as well as if she had never left Guatemala. First the dancing to Latin hip-hop music, and then the language seemed to bridge the gap between Maynor, William, and Bereníce. Or was there something deeper? Did they communicate through a universal bond that only siblings share, like whales conversing across entire oceans in ways that no other mammals understand?

Not just Maynor's pressure but also the thought of losing them again drove her to this nighttime escape, though nothing in her mind, or heart, makes complete sense to her right now. Judy and Ellie have been butting heads ever since they began packing for this trip, and the adoptive mother probably didn't help matters by unequivocally refusing to let the girl visit Tiquisate—an act Bereníce may have perceived as bullheaded and selfish. Yet escaping with her two brothers is not an outright rejection of Judy and Bob, and their love . . . the girl's heart is just torn.

No matter how much time Judy has spent with Ellie since they adopted her, the mother will never truly understand the daughter and the pain she will always carry with her. Sherrie Eldridge touches on that pain in her book *Twenty Things Adopted Kids Wish Their Adoptive Parents Knew*. The book includes chapters titled "My Unresolved Grief May Surface in Anger toward You," "I Need to Know the Truth about My Conception, Birth, and Family History, No Matter How Painful the Details May Be," "I May Appear More 'Whole' Than I Actually Am: I Need Your Help to Uncover the Parts of Myself That I Keep Hidden So I Can Integrate All the Elements of My Identity," "Let Me Be My Own Person . . . but Don't Let Me Cut Myself Off from You," and, especially apt for this situation, "Even If I Decide to Search for My Birth Family, I Will Always Want You to Be My Parents." Quite naturally, though, Judy feels terribly betrayed tonight.

It is well after dark when the runaways disembark in dangerous, seedy

Escuintla at around seven at night, and they have an easy time finding the next chicken bus, toward Santa Lucia, halfway to Tiquisate on the Pacific highway. Bereníce is in good hands with Maynor and William, who know this route well and would never let anything happen to her. To the potential thieves and murderers all around them, they look just like three normal Guatemalan siblings. No reason to mess with them.

Wagner's place is off in the jungle among the coconut and mango trees, and Maynor, William, and Bereníce have to wait a couple of hours in Santa Lucia for a minibus that goes out in his direction. The boys are smart enough not to attempt the journey of several kilometers down the rutted dirt roads toward their mother's boyfriend's land in the dark. They finally arrive at eleven thirty at night, about a half hour after I last called Wagner, and he would later claim that he was surprised to see them. He didn't expect Maynor to follow through with his plan to "escape with Bereníce." And he would say that he didn't have any prepaid minutes left on his cellular phone to call me and let me know that they had sought refuge with him.

The three siblings are exhausted from the journey and the emotional triumph of eluding Judy, and almost immediately they claim the lone bed in Wagner's shack, an old and probably flea-ridden mattress. He moves outside to the hammock, which is strung between two banana trees, and lies awake half the night, keeping watch for anyone who might come and try to take Bereníce away: in other words, us.

Inside, the girl feels hot in her dark jeans and black sweatshirt, and she moves to the bathroom to change into a T-shirt and her short-shorts, the same ones Judy hated because they prompted catcalls in Antigua. But when Bereníce returns, Maynor also tells her they are too skimpy and asks her to put her jeans back on. He is her older brother, and it is his job to protect her. Bereníce returns a second time to the bed and lies down to fall sound asleep between her brothers. At some point in the night Maynor hugs Bereníce and tells her how happy he is that she has returned with them, and that he doesn't want her to go. "Yo tampoco," she answers. Me neither. Bereníce just doesn't want to see Maynor cry again.

꙳

But of course Judy isn't going to return to the United States on Thursday without Ellie. She is her daughter, Bob's daughter, and sister to Amelia and Elizabeth. "Oh, how hurt they are going to feel that Ellie ran away from everything we've given her," Judy mourns. At this moment she is unable to be pragmatic and acknowledge that the girl is just incredibly confused right now. She's lost between two worlds and feels happy that she has rediscovered her Guatemalan family. That doesn't mean she doesn't love Judy and her American family. It just means that in spirit, Ellie is *here* right now and not *there*. But Judy does concede one thing: "I actually feel relieved now that we know there was a plan, and those kids are not lying in a ditch somewhere."

We know we'll find them. Maynor, and William are poor and they don't have many resources. I know Tiquisate, and I know where Antonia lives, where they'll have to go eventually. They won't be able to hide from us for long.

The mother's mood has changed since we talked to Maritza and confirmed the news of their escape. Judy doesn't feel desperate anymore, but upset, and determined. "Those little shits. I'm going to ring their necks when we find them."

We won't wait until tomorrow, or for further news from Antonia and Maritza. Judy and I still aren't convinced that they managed to catch one of the last chicken buses for Escuintla on Monday evening, and so we reserve hope that the three kids may be huddled in a doorway somewhere in the terminal, waiting for the 4:00 a.m. bus out of town. Back at La Capilla, the Canadian hotel managers, Alex and Noel, spring to our aid and make a fresh pot of coffee. We jump into Alex's pickup truck and head for the bus terminal at 1:00 a.m. to comb the streets, asking everyone we come across if they've seen three teenagers—two boys and a girl—in hooded Gap sweatshirts. No sign. They must have made it out Monday afternoon, or they saw the pickup coming and are hiding from us.

We resort to Plan B, a move we never could have imagined just hours ago. We talk to a taxi driver working the graveyard shift in front of the Antigua market and ask him to drive us to the southern coast tomorrow at 4:00 a.m. One-way or round-trip? he asks. No, we'll need his services the entire day. We negotiate a whopping price of one hundred dollars.

Exhausted but determined, Judy and I return to the hotel to catch an hour and a half of restless sleep. The reunion this weekend has been one heck of a culmination of an epic journey, but what right did we have to think the journey was coming to an end? In many ways, for Ellie it is just beginning. And so at ten minutes to four on Tuesday morning, long before sunrise, Judy and I are out on the street waiting for our cab. The town is quiet except for a few dogs barking. Judy is going to save Ellie from making what she calls the worst decision of her daughter's young life.

❧

Our cab driver senses the importance of this mission from the way Judy and I talk back and forth, though we don't reveal much about what's going on. He pushes the gas pedal and makes good time, and at six, just as the sun begins to rise, we are knocking on the door of Maritza and Antonia's house next to the cemetery and the abandoned dilapidated railroad tracks in Rio Bravo. Antonia has just risen from her bed a moment before the knock, and she is still rubbing sleep from her eyes when she unlocks the latch and opens the door, surprised to see Judy in front of her.

"No, no, I have no idea where they are," she says, looking every bit as frustrated as Ellie's other mother. "I didn't sleep a wink last night out of worry for my kids."

We follow her inside, where she begins to make fresh tortillas. Just to be sure, I look around the house to make sure no one is hiding, but other than Antonia, Maritza, Mincho, and Erik who are still sleeping, the place is empty. We sit down on one of the beds, which converts into a makeshift sofa during the day, and discuss what to do next.

"I'm so angry at my boys for running off with Berenice," Antonia proclaims, her eyes reflecting a fiery glow that shows she is wide awake. "When we catch them I'm going to give them a good whopping." And she holds her hands apart as if she were holding an adolescent in her left and a paddle in her right.

"Maritza and I talked, and I understand that she's not mine anymore—Berenice—even though I gave birth to her. She's your daughter, Judy, and I'm going to help you find her."

What a dramatic about-face for this woman Judy has pitied for so long for her poverty, her low self-esteem, her prostitution, her selling of children. Now Judy will place her complete faith in Antonia to reunite her with Ellie. She decides that we should take Antonia with us to Tiquisate and search high and low for any sign of the runaways. Their places to hide are limited, and they'll show up there eventually, if they haven't already. We don't yet know that the kids are with Wagner in the jungle because no one has communicated with him since yesterday evening.

The first stop is a roadside tortilla shack on Tiquisate's main street where Ellie's aunt, Esvin's sister, lives. This is within spitting distance of the house that Antonia built with the money she got from selling the first three babies: the house that Esvin stole and where he lives now with his new woman. We know the place well from photos, and from memories. But Judy and I stay in the cab across the street from the tortilla stand and ask Antonia not to let anyone know we are here. If the kids are nearby, they might run if they see us. Or any number of Esvin's family might be in cahoots with Maynor and William. It's best if no one knows a full-scale search-and-rescue mission is under way.

Antonia returns to the taxi after chatting for five minutes. No sign of them.

The next stop is the house down the dirt path from the Pollo Ranchero fried chicken restaurant where Esvin's parents live. The semitruck for transporting bananas is still there, and I remember that my own journey to locate Ellie's past began on this same corner in late September when I met Jaimes Sr. and Jr. Antonia climbs out of the right-rear door of the cab and knocks on the door of her onetime in-laws' house.

We are descending deeper and deeper into Esvin's world, and it gives us the jitters. Would Maynor bring Ellie to him? Would he hide her from the gringos, maybe even asking for a ransom to get her back? These thoughts are farfetched and probably illogical, yet they do cross Judy's mind. Esvin's parents aren't home, and Antonia returns without clues about the runaways' whereabouts. Worse, a couple kids staring out the window of the house see Judy and me sitting in the cab. The secret is as good as out now, and this might make it much more difficult to locate Ellie.

One last option: we drive through town and turn off onto an even tougher dirt road, through La Shalom where Antonia and the boys used to live, and deeper into a poor colony of shantytowns. We are going to visit Guadalupe, the love of Maynor's life. If he's communicated with anyone in Tiquisate since last night, he's certainly phoned her. But Judy can't sit still in the cab, and when a pretty young girl in a purple dress, shoeless, and with her hair hanging down over her back comes out onto the makeshift porch and meets Antonia, the restless mother jumps out of the taxi and joins Antonia. But again, no sign.

❧

At eight we decide to turn around and head for Santa Lucia to Wagner's place. It's a good hour away and off the beaten path, but we have Antonia on our side, sitting in the backseat holding Judy's hand, and she'll guide us there. We are driving north, through Tiquisate's main street, past the chaotic market and bus terminal where the everyday bustle of people has begun, when I get a phone call despite the spotty cell reception. It's Wagner, and he's sorry he couldn't reach me earlier. The kids are with him, safe and sound, and Berenice is next to him. She wants to talk to me.

The sound of my saying the word *Ellie* and then speaking in clear and present English nearly makes Judy jump out of her seat in the back of the taxi. She nearly rips the phone out of my hand, and I don't resist. But Judy also initially fears that she might be dealing with a hostage situation, and the way to do that is with calm and compassion.

"Ellie," she says, "are you all right?"

She's fine, just exhausted and, from the tone of her voice, a bit relieved that the chase is nearly over.

"I'm so glad you called. We have been very worried about you."

"I know, Mom. I'm really sorry."

"Listen, we're not angry at you, just happy to hear that you are okay, you and your brothers. Now, please stay at Wagner's house. Don't go anywhere. We're coming to meet you, and we'll be there in under an hour."

Judy maintains her composure, though truthfully she is as upset as she is hurt, eased only by the lack of sleep that has put her in a sort of dream state. "I know you're going through a tough time, baby. I know you don't want to say good-bye to your brothers. I know you love them very much. Just wait for us to get there, and we'll talk about things. We don't have to make any quick decisions. Afterwards, we can even come and visit Tiquisate like you wanted."

Antonia takes the telephone next and begins to lecture Maynor in a harsh tone I have not heard her use before. "No, no, Antonia." Judy motions with both hands. "We have to be nice to them and tell them everything is okay, so they don't run away again. Just tell him to stay where they are." We reach the Pacific highway, turn right toward Escuintla, and tell the taxi driver to step on it.

Judy is able to relax a bit as we zoom through the coastal lowlands and past the forests of bananas and sugarcane. We've got them now, and they aren't going to keep running. The only trick will be convincing Ellie to say good-bye to her brothers and get in the cab with us (unless someone pulls out a machete and tries to fight, which is unlikely).

Of course, she is oversimplifying matters in her sleep-deprived state. There is no way what happens next will be easy, especially not on the poor girl known dually as Ellie and Berenice.

It takes us a good hour to get to Santa Lucia and then navigate the labyrinth of washed-out dirt roads leading to Wagner's house. Antonia keeps pointing with her hands, either to the left or to the right, to give directions even though she is seated in the back behind the driver, and he keeps making wrong turns as a result. But, sure enough, by around nine Antonia beckons him to stop next to a little embankment, and the two mothers hop out of the car before it has even come to a halt and scramble up the slope with the agility of teenagers. I slowly get out of the car and tell the driver to take a well-deserved nap, saying, "We may be here a while," and I follow Antonia and Judy down the dirt path toward Wagner's one-room brick house, maybe fifty feet from the road, which is surrounded by beautiful banana and mango trees. Paradise.

Sitting on a wooden bench next to a *pila* cistern in front of the house are Maynor, William, Wagner, and Bereníce, waiting patiently for us. I clear the embankment just as Judy reaches her daughter and embraces her in a fantastic hug. But the girl cannot reciprocate. She is torn between her adoptive mother and her brothers. Judy takes Ellie gently by the hand into the house where they can talk, but the girl keeps looking to her right, out the open doorway, at Maynor and William, whom Antonia has approached and is giving hell for running away without telling anyone.

I catch up to the scene and walk into the house, just as Judy holds out and unfolds Ellie's American passport, the midmorning sunlight illuminating the white eagle on the document's blue background.

"Ellie, do you really want to give up this and everything it stands for—your education, your future, your sisters, your dad and me—and return to this poverty in Guatemala? Do you really want that? Because if you stay here now, you'll be throwing it all away, everything you have been given and everything you have accomplished since we adopted you."

Judy will never forget the completely blank look that comes over the girl's face at that moment, standing on the dirt floor of a one-room brick house in the middle of the jungle, surrounded outside by the love that reared her and then abandoned her, and staring straight at the woman who has given her shelter, and love, and that dark-blue passport, one of the most arrogant symbols of wealth in the world today. Judy is tired, desperate, and hurt, and she may not realize that she's playing the role of imperialist.

Ellie resists the obvious urge to turn her head to the right and look out into the sunshine at the woman who gave birth to her and the brothers with whom she grew up. Instead, she focuses on Judy. "I don't know, Mom. I don't know what to do." A long pause, and then, "Can you make the decision for me?"

Of course the decision will be made for her. Of course Judy's was not an open-ended question. Of course the girl will return to the United States with Judy on Thursday. Whether she likes it or not, she is Ellie Walters. She lives in Traverse City, Michigan, in a nice two-story house on Old Mission Peninsula. She attends sixth grade at Traverse City Central, excels on the junior high girls' basketball team, and attends summer camp at the prestigious Interlochen Arts Academy where she is a voice major. And yes, she owns that American passport with the eagle on it—the document coveted by so many.

The match today here in this jungle in Central America was not going to be fair. In fact, it was fixed to begin with. Two poor Guatemalan boys with no money, no resources, and no valuable passports never really stood a chance against a middle-class white woman from the United States when it came to fighting over the fourteen-year-old girl they all love and need so badly. At the end of this week, Guatemala's most valuable natural resources, its children, will still be leaving the country on airplanes for *El Norte*, and this particular case will be no different. At the end of the month, Guatemala's role will still be one of subservience to the United States of America.

Outside, Maynor has picked up a knife and is carving into a ripe mango he plucked from the tree. The blade cuts open the fruit, but the juices bleed all over his hands, the process messy. He pleads to anyone who will listen: Antonia, Wagner, even me. "Ella no quiere salir." She told me she doesn't want to go. She wants to stay here with us. And that familiar impressionable look of marvel comes over Antonia's face again as she turns and looks at us gringos as if she expects us to answer Maynor with a sparring of words. It's the same look she gave when we told her Ellie was in sixth grade and liked to sing and draw, the same look on her face when the doctor told her two days ago that if she didn't have a hysterectomy she would probably die; it could be the same look on her face after Doña Cesy told her to give up her seven-year-old girl all those years ago.

"He says Bereníce doesn't want to go," Antonia tells us, nodding toward Maynor.

At that the translator-narrator uneasily sheds the remnants of his objectivity, knowing that the outcome has already been decided—it just needs to be justified. "Antonia, Bereníce is very confused. She's a fragile fourteen-year-old girl, and she's torn between her Guatemalan and American families. She doesn't know what's best for her right now."

There is no response from Maynor, and Antonia just stares.

"You will see Bereníce many times during your lifetimes." The voice is directed toward Maynor and William. "She will come back and visit often, I'm sure. She loves you, and you are an important part of her life. This is only good-bye for a little while. You are not losing her the way you did the last time."

William is bowing his head and nodding silently, as if he is sorry for their actions, but Maynor has dropped the mango and the carving knife and retreated to the bench, where he holds his head in his hands, crying hard.

By now Judy and Ellie have left the house and are standing in the crowd. The narrator backs up a few steps and addresses the crowd, repeating the question in both Spanish and English several times so everyone understands: "This girl belongs to both of your families. She is both Guatemalan and American, and she will probably spend her life going back and forth between these two countries. She loves all of you and needs all of you equally. But for her to be happy, those that love her need to be willing to share her, even if that means knowing you won't see her all the time. Who here loves this girl so much that they are willing to share her? *Levanta la mano.* Raise your hand!"

First William and Judy simultaneously answer the call, their right hands shooting up into the air. A moment later Wagner does, and he nudges Antonia, who might not have completely understood the question, but raises her hand nonetheless. Sadly, it is only Maynor, sulking, defeated, on the bench, a day shy of returning to the banana *finca* and probably less than a year away from marrying Guadalupe, who doesn't respond.

The girl looks around the crowd, at her brother, her two mothers, and Wagner, arms all bent at the elbow and raised, and though her back is turned to me, I think she smiles.

❧

Ellie will get her wish. Before returning home she will see Tiquisate, the village where she was born and she knew intimately, even though she mistakenly thought it was in El Salvador. She will sweat in its heat, know its faces, and see its bustling poverty.

Ellie gets into the back of the taxicab and sits between Antonia, to her left, and Judy, to her right, though today she favors her Guatemalan mother and holds her hand while ignoring her American mother. This would deeply hurt Judy, even though she knows deep down that Ellie is just confused. "Once I get her back to the United States, in a few days she'll warm up to me and she'll be ours once again," Judy tells herself. I climb into the passenger seat and slap the dusty dashboard to awaken the sleeping driver. He looks around him and smiles when he sees Ellie in the backseat. His sheepish grin seems to say, "So this is the reason we've been driving around the country all morning."

The driver shakes his head, starts the engine, and returns to the highway and then back to Tiquisate. Judy, Ellie, and I are sound asleep when Antonia asks the driver to stop in front of the tortilla stand near her old house on the town's main street, where we stopped earlier this morning to look for the runaways. Since then, she has figured out how to give directions from the backseat. The three of us awake to the sound of Antonia's jubilant voice: "I want to introduce Berenice to the rest of her family before she leaves."

We climb out of the taxi, cross the street, and accept the plastic chairs offered to us under a plastic tarp that keeps out at least some of the scorching sun. Ellie's aunt, Esvin's sister, offers us refreshing cups of purified water, and says how happy she is to see the girl again, but how equally proud she feels to know that Ellie has a good life in the United States. We give the woman a couple of quetzales to buy a plastic bag of freshly cooked tortillas, some of the best we've ever tasted, and at that moment a little old lady who can't be more than four feet tall hobbles over to us. Her skin is worn and leathery, and she appears to be missing quite a few teeth, but her smile is warm and gentle, as is her handshake. This is Ellie's grandmother Rosa, Esvin's mother.

By now she has heard about last night's daring escape, and she wags her bony finger and gives Ellie a kind, grandmotherly scolding for the adventure. Why would she give up a life in *the United States*? the woman asks. Then Grandmother Rosa turns to Judy and tells her how grateful she is for all the woman has done for this lucky girl. "Suerte," she repeats. Lucky. Antonia stands next to Ellie's grandmother, beaming with pride the entire time.

We drive on and stop at the Tiquisate bus terminal because Ellie wants to see the teeming market, one of the places she remembered well from her birth village. This is where she would sweep the floors for a few quetzales during those tough days after her father abandoned them and before she was given up for adoption. We are just about to duck down one of the many paths descending into the market when Antonia suddenly exclaims, "Mira, Esvin." Look, there's Esvin. And standing in front of us, leaning against a wooden pole that is holding up the plastic tarp roof, is the character that this story had forgotten.

Esvin Arnoldo Ortiz Gonzalez, thirty-six years old, the father of Maynor, William, and Berenice and the other four children Antonia gave up for adoption; the man who favored the bottle of *aguardiente* over his children, stole Antonia's house, and kicked them all out onto the street in favor of another woman; the man who stands before us now, wobbling as if he's drunk, a five o'clock shadow and eyes that suggest a hangover, and wearing a filthy checkered shirt covered with food stains. We were afraid of this man because we didn't know what he'd do to Antonia, or Ellie, or the boys. But at this moment he looks helpless and pathetic. Antonia doesn't fear him; she doesn't even hate him any longer, as she tells us afterward. The way she addresses him, the way she introduces him to his daughter, shows that she just pities him.

Esvin shakes Ellie's hand, quickly and without affection, though he acknowledges he knows who she is and then mumbles a few inaudible words. He shakes Judy's hand and mine too, and before turning and stumbling away into the market he says, "I did what I could for the girl. I wish I could have done more."

It all happens in a flash, and moments later he is gone . . . for Ellie, and for the story, a distant memory once again. Nearly doubled over with fatigue from the heat and lack of sleep, Judy, Ellie, and Antonia do not dwell on meeting Esvin and don't even exchange words about him. Instead, they move on to the next event in this whirlwind tour of Berenice's past. Yet the birth father's appearance today was so sudden and seemingly insignificant that it spoke volumes.

Our final stop in Tiquisate is to the clapboard shack a block away from the market where Antonia and her kids lived after Esvin abandoned them, where Antonia resorted to prostitution to make money, and where Cesy and Estela courted her to sell her children. We know this house from the photos Maynor took on the first day we met him last fall: the fading blue paint on the *pila* out front, the *jocote* tree with scuff marks in it where the kids used to play. Antonia hasn't been here in a while, but the neighbors do remember her, and one older woman even remembers Ellie, the girl who they figured had died. At our request, they give us a tour of the rooms where the family once lived. Two little boys without shoes scratch their heads from what could be head lice while swinging in a hammock inside a dark room. Absolute, grinding poverty, and Ellie is absorbing it all.

The family is honored by our visit, and they offer us chairs and drinks. But Judy can tell that Ellie no longer feels comfortable in this setting, and she suggests that we get back in the taxi, drop off Antonia, and head for Antigua. On the way out the door, Ellie says to her American mom, "I don't really like Tiquisate. I'm more of an Antigua kind of girl," and Judy shoots me a sigh of relief because she knows what that ultimately means. In its wealth and decadence, Antigua is America, not Guatemala.

By the time we return to Maritza's house in Rio Bravo, Maynor and William are there as well, having caught a bus from Wagner's place. For Ellie that means saying good-bye all over again, but the kids are somewhat deflated from last night's adventures, and after twenty minutes and a bucketful of tears we are able to get her back in the taxi. A last-minute decision is made that William will accompany us back to Antigua because he wants to study at Safe Passage and the director, Hanley Denning, seemed open to the possibility of his replacing Maynor. William has no girlfriend or church affiliation holding him back in Tiquisate, and we hope he can move into the Casa Hogar and begin studying very soon.

Judy and Ellie both promise that they'll return again soon, and Antonia, the hero of the day for finding Berenice and bringing her back to Judy, is the last one to hug the girl before we close the doors of the taxi. We head east, along the Pacific highway and its sugarcane and banana fields and aroma of fermenting fruit, before turning north for the ascent into the highlands, the valley of the volcanoes, and finally Antigua—a route quite familiar to us all by now.

Eleanor Patricia Berenice Ortiz sleeps soundly in the backseat with her Guatemalan brother William sitting to her left and her American adoptive mother, Judy, to her right. Her journey has come full circle, and on Thursday she will return to Michigan, and the sixth grade.

❧ Epilogue

Ellie Walters returned to her typical teenage lifestyle in Traverse City, Michigan, in mid-February 2006—as typical as the frenetic life of a fourteen year old can be, that is—though the reunion with her birth family the week before clearly changed her forever. She thought about Antonia, Maynor, and William constantly during those first few nights at home on Old Mission Peninsula, and Judy wrote me that Ellie was experiencing a mild form of post-trip depression. Ellie's sentiments fitted the analysis of Betty Jean Lifton: "Adoptees who have taken the journey through Search and Reunion know that what is lost can be found, but never fully recovered. It comes back to us in new forms, but never in the shape of what might have been. And though we feel complete in knowing our story, in being grounded, we cannot say that the integrating process is ever concluded. It may take the lifetime left to absorb."

Ellie mourned, especially for Maynor, who was beside himself with grief for days after his sister left Tiquisate again, even as he returned to work on the banana plantation and talked of marrying his girlfriend, Guadalupe. Ellie waited anxiously for news about William, who entered the Safe Passage program in Antigua and began school again a week later. She also worried about Antonia, who refused to go to the local public hospital and sign up for a hysterectomy. Her uterus pains came and went, depending on whether Wagner had enough money to pay for the medicine recommended by a different doctor in Tiquisate.

Despite the pain Judy felt when Ellie ran off into the jungle, the adoptive mother confirmed that their future (for both her and Bob) would certainly include Antonia's family, now that such a tight bond was established, even though she admitted that "it truly would have been easier and fine with me if this trip had taken care of business for Ellie."

Judy weathered torrents of criticism from family and friends for taking Ellie back to Guatemala to meet her past. Colleagues at work told her that fourteen was simply way too early, while Judy's in-laws believed that a reunion at any time in the girl's life was a big mistake. Why reopen those old wounds? they would ask. Let bygones be bygones, echoing the traditional philosophy of burying the past to protect an adopted child. Of course, Judy's telling them about Ellie's escape into the jungle with her two brothers merely added fuel to their fire. But Judy became defensive and wrote me that these people just didn't understand why Ellie needed this. "My family doesn't get why I felt she needed the contact with a mother who gave her up. . . . Our love for her includes her need for her roots. Her contact with Antonia has forever healed her from the abandoned, left-on-the-doorstep trauma that most adopted people have to wrestle with."

Of course, Judy and Bob had to deal with the painful rejection they felt because Ellie, for one dramatic night at least, chose her brothers and Guatemala over her adoptive family, her sisters, and the United States. But Judy and Bob are self-confident, mature adults who are able to understand and accept how complicated teenagers can be, in any country. Within days of returning home, Ellie apologized for "excluding [Judy] whenever her Mother [Antonia] was around." The girl had preferred to hold Antonia's hand instead of Judy's hand in the Parque Central in Antigua and in the taxicab in Tiquisate. Eventually, Ellie decided that they could just refer to her as "Mother Antonia" so as not to leave anyone out.

Bob woke up one morning and said, "I'm not mad, but somewhat disappointed in her. But geez . . . how can you be disappointed in someone who wants to be with family?" Judy and Bob discussed how the reunion had turned out and concluded that they didn't regret taking Ellie back to Guatemala. "We have always allowed her the possibility of going back . . . She just chose to do it sooner than we wanted," he added.

As for Ellie's twin sisters, they took the news of Ellie's escape into the jungle with ease, and that surprised Judy. "It was interesting how supportive Amelia and Elizabeth were of Ellie," she wrote to me. "They didn't seem to feel hurt or betrayed or any lack of loyalty from her. Any conspiracy against authority [parents] is applauded in their adolescent minds."

And so their lives as teenagers continued. Ellie returned to the sixth grade and amazed her whole class with stories from her dramatic trip back to Guatemala. In the evenings she would think about Maynor rising at four in the morning to load bananas into trucks all day and William opening books again for the first time since he was a small boy, but her mind would also return to still-wintry northern Michigan as she stared out the window at the basketball hoop in a nearby driveway and wished the snow away. Ellie applied for and won a voice scholarship to return to the prestigious Interlochen Arts Academy the following summer. And two months after the reunion she traveled with Bob to New Orleans to help in the relief effort after Hurricane Katrina.

Ellie still talked about making a lot of money once she finishes school so that she could return to Guatemala and build a big house for her family so they wouldn't have to suffer any longer. She believed that in the future she would spend plenty more time with Antonia, Maynor, and William, her older sister Maritza, and her two nephews, Mincho and Erik, and even Antonia's boyfriend, Wagner. But Ellie felt no need to meet her biological father, Esvin, again.

৵

Within a year of the reunion the lives of the Guatemalans had settled into the kind of mundane calm that one finds in rural poverty. Maynor never married Guadalupe, and instead hitched up with another girl, named Haidi, who became pregnant with his child. The subsequent fight between Haidi's parents, Maynor, and his older sister Maritza sent Antonia, Maynor, and Wagner packing, to a little shack made of tin sheet metal, on the land near Santa Lucia where Judy and I found Ellie and her brothers the morning after their escape. Haidi gave birth to a little girl a year after the reunion, and Maynor wouldn't meet her for another year after that. For a time, he found steady work in a chicken factory near their hut, where he packaged poultry that is exported all over the world. Though the work was tedious and unchallenging, Maynor was proud of the company-authorized uniform and hairnet he wore, and before being let go, he dutifully brought home his monthly salary of fifteen hundred quetzales (around two hundred dollars) for Antonia.

William stuck it out at the Safe Passage school in Antigua for almost a year, despite several attempts to escape and return to Tiquisate to be with his family. During that year he completed the equivalent of two years in his studies, and the directors of the program convinced Judy to pay extra for private tutoring, since they considered William one of their brightest students. Ultimately, though, William submitted to the shame he felt for not earning money to help his mother and for the mental and physical abuse he suffered at Safe Passage at the hands of older and tougher boys his age who had grown up on the mean streets of the Guatemala City garbage dump. By early 2007 William had returned to the lowlands to be with Antonia and Maynor, though he still held out hope that he could attend school somewhere near Santa Lucia, with Judy's financial support.

Sadly, Safe Passage suffered a mighty blow in January 2007 when its founder, Hanley Denning, dubbed the "angel of the garbage dump" by the Guatemalan press, was killed in a car crash between Antigua and Guatemala City. Her funeral procession seemed to stretch from the depths of the garbage dump all the way to her home state of Maine, and touched thousands of people along the way. Hanley was recognized in the U.S. Congress and by then first lady Laura Bush during a visit to Safe Passage, and for weeks after her death the *Portland Press Herald* in Maine ran nonstop coverage of her devotion to Safe Passage.

Judy Barrett was so touched by Hanley's life and death, and what she did for Maynor and William, that she flew to Maine for the funeral and continues to play an active role in the Great Lakes Friends of Safe Passage, one of several chapters of the organization that have sprung up all over the United States. In the spring of 2007 the program hired a new director, and it continues to offer families a path out of the city garbage dump.

ꝍ

At the requests of both Antonia and Judy, I launched a search for Erik, the brother of Ellie, Maynor, and William who was also given up for adoption sometime in the mid- to late 1990s, although Antonia didn't remember the exact dates, and, unlike Judy, she hadn't saved any paperwork over the years. But she did remember the name and telephone number of the attorney in Guatemala City who facilitated Erik's adoption, and she remembered the lawyer, Señor Jorge Vidrio, telling her that Erik would be sent to live with a French family. As Antonia tells it, that family contacted Vidrio and actually returned to Guatemala City after adopting Erik with the intention of finding and meeting Antonia.

A beautiful coincidence, I thought. Like Judy, Bob, and Ellie in the United States, there was a family in France who wanted to establish a link from the present to the past for their son (who may well have a different name today).

But Antonia was in El Salvador when the family arrived, and she didn't learn of Vidrio's phone calls to Tiquisate until they had already returned to France. She was given only the picture of Erik, happy and healthy, skiing on a snowy surface. After she was reacquainted with Ellie, Antonia desperately wanted news of what had happened to Erik, the boy she gave up as a four year old. There were three others she relinquished as infants, of course, but Antonia didn't recall which lawyers facilitated those adoptions, and today those kids, wherever they are, would have no memories of Guatemala. And Maynor, William, Ellie, and Erik never even knew them.

Finding Jorge Vidrio in Guatemala City wasn't difficult. He was an old man by the time I tracked him down, and he no longer worked with adoptions because, he told me, the business isn't so lucrative anymore. But when I did my homework on Vidrio I discovered a lot of dirt. A woman from California who had e-mailed me on a whim when she learned I was writing a book about Guatemalan adoption knew of Jorge Vidrio. In fact, he had facilitated her adoption of a girl named Maria who was now a teenager and living in the Bay Area, but when she and her daughter returned to Guatemala several years ago to locate and meet her birth mother, they showed up in the rural village and learned that the legal birth mother listed in Maria's dossier was actually the true birth mother's sister-in-law, who stole Maria from her husband's sister's arms and sold the girl to Vidrio, who apparently forged the documents.

I met Jorge Vidrio on two occasions—at a seafood restaurant near the Tikal Futura mall in Guatemala City, where he drank one beer after another, whistled at the pretty waitresses young enough to be his granddaughters, and then expected me to pick up the entire tab, and at his office in the same building as a well-known strip club in a gritty part of the capital. Needless to say, I was careful not to corner him and threaten him, or criticize his line of work. I didn't tell him I was writing a book about Guatemalan adoption, only that I was a close friend of the family who had adopted one of Juana Antonia Cubillas Rodrigues's other children, and that we were interested in tracking down Erik in France. Luckily, I don't think Vidrio ever suspected me of having an ulterior motive. I didn't want to end up like that Casa Alianza lawyer who had been gunned down on his way to work six months earlier.

Miraculously, Vidrio still had Antonia's Salvadoran passport from her relinquishment of Erik probably a decade earlier, and he handed it over to me without a question so I could return it to her. He did have a phone number for an adoption contact in rural France, who probably knew the family that now has Erik, but the number was extremely outdated, and calls to France have yet to bear fruit.

❧

In the late summer of 2007, as the floor began to crumble under what had become the most productive adoption industry in the world, a sense of anxious dread overcame the community of Americans in Antigua, in Guatemala City, and on Web sites like GuatAdopt.com, who were waiting to adopt and bring their children home. The State Department issued several warnings, each one more ominous than the last, urging Americans not to begin the process of adopting from Guatemala. On August 11, the paranoia reached a fever pitch when Guatemalan governmental authorities—likely with First Lady Wendy Berger acting behind the scenes—raided the adoption foster home that I've called by the pseudonym "Hogar Nuevo Día," where Ellie Walters lived before her adoption. Citing suspicions of "irregularities" in the adoption process, the authorities occupied the home and seized forty-two kids waiting to be adopted and placed them initially in homes that don't focus on adoption. The raid sent shock waves through the adoption community, both in Guatemala and in the United States, and inspired hundreds of nervous postings on GuatAdopt.com.

In early December, the Ortega law passed the Guatemala Congress, nearly unanimously, spelling the end of privatized notary adoptions. And a week later, while Christmas shopping in Chicago on December 15, I finally got a call from the man I'd been trying to track down, via telephone or e-mail, for more than two years: in this book I've called him Clayton Phelpers, the head of "Hogar Nuevo Día," and one of the first Americans to get rich through the Guatemalan adoption industry. Having been mostly demonized in the media since his foster home was raided four months earlier (likely bringing his work with international adoption to a close), Phelpers launched an obscenity-laden tirade at me for an article I had published in the magazine *In These Times*, which implicated him and his wife, the attorney whom I've called "Cassandra Arriba," for bribing and tricking Antonia into relinquishing Ellie. Phelpers denied any premeditation with respect to the *jaladoras* who recruited Antonia to bring Ellie to Antigua in

1999, claiming that she was officially "abandoned" and not voluntarily relinquished. He ended the conversation with the firm conviction that if the girl hadn't been given up for adoption, she would have become a prostitute in the streets.

It's difficult to predict what will happen with Guatemalan adoption since grinding to a halt in the fall of 2008. Will it go the way of other Latin America and Eastern European countries and all but shut down now that the government (and its ugly twin, bureaucracy) has wrested control of the process away from the efficient, yet profit-driven, attorneys? Or will the massive lobbying effort that Guatemalan adoption attorneys and adoption agencies here in the United States have launched (often in collaboration) somehow reopen the window, even though Guatemala has passed the Ortega law and eliminated the privatized notary system?

With the power to grant adoptions in Guatemala now in the hands of the government, and the U.S. State Department placing a freeze on subsequent cases, no new children are coming to the United States—down from nearly five thousand during the 2007 fiscal year. For better or worse, the responsibility for that drastic change falls squarely on the shoulders of the Guatemalan Congress, UNICEF, and dignitaries like former first lady Wendy Berger. Many call it a massive tragedy to deprive so many children of families who can offer them health care, education, three meals a day, and, yes, prom nights and iPods too. Others will call this the closure of another chapter in the United States' long history of imperialism over Guatemala. As evidence they'll cite the assumption that life in America is automatically superior to life in Guatemala—the point expressed by Judy when she flaunted Ellie's blue passport that day in the jungle.

Meanwhile, for better or for worse, Juana Antonia Cubillas Rodrigues would probably still have all ten children under one roof, and Ellie and Erik never would have been separated from Maynor and William, were foreign adoption not an option in Guatemala. Who knows what would have happened to the girl who is now McKenna Hayman in Tennessee? Could her birth mother, Norma, have found a way to raise another child alongside her teenagers, Carlos and Veronica? How would Norma's family have reacted to the news that another affair had ended badly and another baby was on the way? Could McKenna have been happy growing up Aelyn Melissa (her original name) in poor Costa Cuca near the coffee *fincas*—certainly without swimming pools, sweet tea, and all the gifts of wealth and love that April and Kenny Hayman lavish on her?

⁂

Even as Ellie Walters patched up the wounds that were inflicted upon her when she was torn away from Guatemala a second time, I continued to struggle with the depth of my involvement in her journey back for the reunion with Antonia and her biological family.

As soon as I agreed to help Judy find Juana Antonia Cubillas Rodrigues for the purpose of later facilitating a reunion with Ellie, it was obvious to me that I could no longer play the role of a fly-on-the-wall journalist, which had been my intention. And the more time I spent with Antonia and her two sons Maynor and William, and the more I prepped Judy and Ellie for the culture shock they would experience when they visited Guatemala, the more I influenced these characters and how they would eventually interact when they met each other.

Luckily, what dominated Ellie's ultimate reunion with her mother and brothers wasn't so much any dialogue but physical dynamics: those first moments when they embraced again; the night of dancing to hip-hop music when Ellie, Maynor, and William joined hands; and, of course, their dramatic escape into the jungle—painful, but organic and touching scenes that I the documentarian didn't cause, only witnessed.

I played an inherent role in facilitating an emotional and painful reunion for a girl who was only fourteen years old. But I promised myself throughout the nine months I knew Ellie before her reunion with Antonia, Maynor, and William that I would place every decision in the hands of her legal parents, Judy Barrett and Bob Walters, two competent and decent—if at times a little naive—parents and well-educated American citizens who, I believe, understood enough of the dynamics at hand to make intelligent decisions. I didn't push for such an early reunion with Ellie's birth family. That came entirely from Judy, who didn't want to risk losing Antonia to an early death before her daughter could meet her again.

At certain times during my interactions with Judy I felt it necessary to hatch out of my journalist's shell and express concerns about what was happening. Not to do so would have meant betraying her and Ellie as confidantes and friends. There were times when I felt so nervous I wanted to turn around, like the day we took a taxi from Escuintla to Tiquisate for our initial meeting with Antonia, though I downplayed those feelings at the time because, again, I didn't want to influence the outcome of the story.

Judy had asked me if I knew of any other ways to track down and meet the biological mother of one's child, and I mentioned Guatemalan Roots. I had met Blanca Estela from Guatemalan Roots two weeks previous in the capital, and she described to me how delicate this process of reunion was. You're playing with people's lives, she told me. And if you make a mistake and scare the biological mother away once, you close the door forever.

We had met at an Italian restaurant in Guatemala City, and Blanca Estela had spoken with the speed and precision of a judge, choosing her exact words minutes before they actually came out of her mouth. She studied my every move as we sat across from each other, and that made me feel very uncomfortable. When I told her that I, a journalist, not a social worker, planned to wander into poor villages and find the birth mothers of kids in the States—and all I knew about them were names and addresses—the expression on her face betrayed concern.

I can see why. Was it reckless to dive into a strange foreign land where logic and order don't always prevail and where danger lurks around every corner, to facilitate and translate for a climactic and sensitive reunion between a lost girl and the mother who abandoned her even though I'm neither a social worker nor an adoptee, to assume that Ellie Walters would benefit from being reacquainted with her scarred past? It was a little reckless, and naive, but I sincerely believe that, despite the pain, the reunion improved the lives of everyone involved. And if this story helps capture the trauma and complexity of the Guatemalan adoption journey, then it was worth writing.

❧ Bibliography

SOURCES ON LATIN AMERICA AND GUATEMALA

Casa de los babys. Directed by John Sayles. IFC Films, 2003.

Goldman, Francisco. *The Long Night of White Chickens*. New York: Grove Press, 1998.

Goodbye Baby. Directed by Patricia Goudvis. Harriman NY: New Day Films, 2005.

Menchu, Rigoberta. *I, Rigoberta Menchu: An Indian Woman in Guatemala*. New York: Verso, 1984.

Nazario, Sonia. *Enrique's Journey: The Story of a Boy's Dangerous Odyssey to Reunite with His Mother*. New York: Random House, 2005.

Nelson, Diane M. *A Finger in the Wound: Body Politics in Quincentennial Guatemala*. Berkeley: University of California Press, 1999.

Pople, Larissa. "Children as Commodities in a Globalised World: International Adoption in Guatemala." PhD diss., University of London's Institute of Latin American Studies, 2003.

Schlesinger, Stephen, and Stephen Kinzer. *Bitter Fruit: The Story of the American Coup in Guatemala*. Cambridge: Harvard University Press, 1999.

Trenka, Jane Jeong, Julia Chinyere Oparah, and Sun Yung Shin, eds. *Outsiders Within: Writing on Transracial Adoption*. Cambridge MA: South End Press, 2006.

Wilkinson, Daniel. *Silence on the Mountain: Stories of Terror, Betrayal, and Forgetting in Guatemala*. Boston: Houghton Mifflin, 2002.

SOURCES ON FOREIGN ADOPTION

The Adoption History Project. http://darkwing.uoregon.edu/~adoption/. Maintained by Ellen Herman. Eugene: Department of History, University of Oregon.

Eldridge, Sherrie. *Twenty Things Adopted Kids Wish Their Adoptive Parents Knew*. New York: Random House, 1999.

Howell, Signe. *The Kinning of Foreigners: Transnational Adoption in a Global Perspective*. Oxford: Berghahn Books, 2006.

Lifton, Betty Jean. *Journey of the Adopted Self: A Quest for Wholeness*. New York: Basic Books, 1995.

————. *Lost and Found: The Adoption Experience*. New York: HarperCollins, 1988.

Pertman, Adam. *Adoption Nation: How the Adoption Revolution Is Transforming America*. New York: Basic Books, 2001.

Wolkman, Toby Alice, ed. *Cultures of Transnational Adoption*. Durham NC: Duke University Press, 2005.